TEARING DOWN THE CURTAIN

The People's Revolution in Eastern Europe
by a team from *The Observer*

Julie Flint, Nigel Hawkes, Peter Hillmore, Ian Mather,
Mike Power, Denise Searle, John Sweeney, Nick Thorpe

Edited by Nigel Hawkes

Photographs by
Bill Robinson, Roger Hutchings, Dod Miller and Gamma

Hodder & Stoughton

LONDON SYDNEY AUCKLAND TORONTO

Cover photograph (Wenceslas Square, Czechoslovakia):
Roger Hutchings

ISBN 0 340 53617 9

First published 1990

© 1990 The Observer Limited

Typeset by Wearside Tradespools, Fulwell, Sunderland
Printed in Great Britain for Headway, a division of Hodder and
Stoughton Ltd, Mill Road, Dunton Green, Sevenoaks, Kent by
St Edmundsbury Press Ltd, Bury St Edmunds, Suffolk.

CONTENTS

PREFACE

1989 was a year worthy to be ranked with 1789, 1848 or 1917. In a few short months, governments fell across Eastern Europe and a whole structure of relationships and attitudes crumbled. A pattern that had kept Europe secure, if immobile, was replaced by a future full of unimagined possibilities. It happened in a blur; so fast that each event fell successively on sensibilities still trying to absorb the last. It is for this reason that *The Observer* decided to produce an account of the events in Eastern Europe, written by those who observed them at first hand.

The bulk of the book has been written by the eight-strong team listed on the title page. But they have borrowed phrases, descriptions, and judgements supplied by others who have written for *The Observer* over this period. For their felicities, we give our thanks. For our errors, we are alone responsible.

The revolutions of 1789 and 1917 gave way to terror and authoritarianism; those of 1848 were quickly crushed. If 1989 is to be remembered not as a brief moment of hope but as the beginning of a new age of freedom and democracy, people everywhere will have to understand why the people's revolutions came about, and how to build on their success. It is to contribute to that that this book is written.

London, March 1990

The Eastern European illusion

When did the collapse of the Soviet empire in Eastern Europe begin? Some would say from the empire's very start. No empire lasts forever and perhaps the Soviets should take pride in having held on to theirs for 45 years in a century when history has moved so fast. For a while, they even persuaded the rest of the world that Eastern Europe was more than a loose geographical expression. Looking at the Soviet bloc from the West we thought we saw identical political structures; the same economic formulae; and a strident diplomacy conducted in unison from all the East European capitals. They were minor differences but only very occasionally were they significant, like Poland's refusal or inability to collectivise its farming – though theorists in Moscow believed this, too, would only be temporary. In essentials, Eastern Europe from the outside looked for many years what the Soviet leaders wanted it to be: reliably and drearily mono-lithic.

It was an illusion. The six countries occupied by the Soviet army at the end of World War II never had much in common. True, three of them – Poland, Czechoslovakia and Bulgaria – were Slav. Bulgaria, though, was far away in the backward Balkans, Orthodox in religion, and marked by years of Turkish occupation from which even the 19th century Russian tsars had seemed desirable saviours. Catholic Poland and Catholic and Protestant Czechoslovakia, although neighbours, had had difficult relations after their rc-establishment as independent states at the end of World War I. Czechoslovakia, its western regions of Bohemia and Moravia already as developed as anywhere in Germany, was born out of the Habsburg empire and could therefore afford to show some warmth and understanding towards the big Slav brothers in Russia. In 1918 the Poles had escaped from three foreign masters – Austrians, Russians and Germans – and they remained obsessed, rightly it turned out, with the continuing threat posed to Poland's future by the latter two. The German occupation during World War II and the Sovietisation that followed meant for many Poles simply a return to patterns of resistance that had been the country's way of life for the best part of 200 years. In Czechoslovakia, though, many people at first tried to make the most out of the forced alliance with Moscow.

Two countries were *sui generis*. Romania, though Balkan, Orthodox and also like Bulgaria an escapee from Turkish domination, saw itself as a Latin island in a sea of Slavs. While its intellectuals spoke French and dreamed of Paris, everyday life between the two world wars meant keeping up one's guard against the Soviet Communists in the north and the Hungarians to the west. Romanian distrust of both these countries did not vanish in 1945. It went underground.

Hungary felt, and would go on feeling, even more isolated than Romania. A small nation on a territory without natural defences, it could not claim like Romania to be a distant part of a greater patrimony. The award of Transylvania to the Romanians under the peace settlement following World War I would have scarred a much larger and more secure nation. For Hungary, Transylvania's loss and the plight of the Hungarian minority there remained (and remains) a national obsession. When the Communists came to power they declared the subject taboo: one of the Soviet Union's most effective ways of imposing apparent uniformity on the bloc was to ban the media of one country for writing anything unfavourable about another. Hungarian Communists allowed neither themselves nor anyone else critical words about Romania's treatment of the Transylvanian Hungarians. Hungarian resentment therefore also went underground, where it built up a hidden reservoir of bad feeling against not only Romania but also Moscow and the Communist leaders in Budapest for refusing to let Hungarians speak what was on their mind.

As for East Germany, it was of course an absolute odd man out. The five Länder composing it were suddenly deprived of their natural ties with the rest of Germany. How artificial East Germany's place in the Soviet empire was could now be judged by the East German Communists' extravagant efforts to prove that it was both natural and permanent. It was not enough to build a wall to separate themselves from the other Germany. They had to claim that East Germans were evolving into something new, into a socialist nation quite different from the Germans in the West. Whenever there was a crisis in the Soviet bloc brought about by national discontent, the East German leaders were the first to call for a restoration of monolithic, class order. It was not difficult to see that they were trying too hard, and were never as sure of themselves and their new German socialist identity as they wanted the world to believe.

In one important way the Eastern Europe of 1945 was actually less knitted together by common threads than it had been at the beginning of the war. Almost all these countries had, in 1939, large Jewish or German communities, and in some cases both. These communities contributed greatly to cultural and economic life and brought intimations of a wider world into countries that tended to be obsessed by their own problems and identities. This impact was greatest on the cities, where the richest and best-educated Germans and Jews lived. Here, if anywhere, were the makings of a *Mitteleuropa* founded not on rule by empire but on a shared Central European spirit. This common foundation was destroyed by the war and its aftermath. Hitler had killed most of the Jews: they remained as a sizeable community only in Hungary. As for the Germans, most of them were driven out by the newly liberated Eastern European states. Those that managed to stay on, like the Hungarian Germans and the Saxons of Romania, were mainly peasants who kept their heads down. In spite of Communist propaganda about a new international community, the nations of post-war Eastern Europe were essentially inward-looking.

The Russians were able to keep Communism in place in this ill-assorted half dozen countries only as long as they showed readiness to use force. We can now see that each Soviet police action – the suppression of the East German workers' rebellion in 1953, of the Hungarian uprising in 1956 and of the 1968 Prague Spring – demanded ever greater effort while yielding less and less satisfactory results. Soviet officials, looking at Janos Kadar's Hungary, could congratulate themselves that putting down the Hungarian revolt in 1956 had paid off. Within 10 years Hungary seemed to be politically stable. Its living standard was rising. Kadar seemed almost popular. But intelligent Russians soon realised they had not been able to repeat the trick in Czechoslovakia. The Communist leaders who replaced Alexander Dubcek after 1968 never won back the confidence of the nation. And then came December 1981, when the peaceful and measured Polish uprising led by Solidarity was put down not by Soviet troops but by the Warsaw authorities themselves. General Jaruzelski's action followed months of brow-beating of the Poles by Soviet marshals, Politburo members and a posse of lesser apparatchiks.

At the time it seemed proof that Moscow was as determined as ever to keep its empire intact, and that it would allow no political deviation that might put the empire's survival in question, above all no watering down of the Communist Party's absolute authority. But the obvious fact was the most important one. Not a single Soviet soldier crossed the Polish frontier ready to do combat. The Poles did Moscow's job for it.

Wasn't there a special explanation for that? Poles, including Polish soldiers, would probably have fought on a large scale against a Soviet intervention. The Soviet marshals certainly had no appetite for such a fight, not least because it would take place on their lines of communication with the 380,000-strong Soviet army in East Germany. But there were other considerations, too. The Soviet army was already struggling in Afghanistan, with considerable damage to Moscow's international relationship with the West. A Soviet invasion of Poland that triggered off yet another doomed Polish uprising would have destroyed for the foreseeable future any chance of advantageous agreements on arms control and economic relations with the West. It is doubtful that the Soviet leaders fully understood their inhibitions about going into Poland in 1980, but somewhere at the back of their minds they seem to have perceived that the world was changing. What Moscow could do in Hungary in 1956, and in Czechoslovakia 12 years later, could not be repeated in Poland in 1980.

It took another five years, and the appearance of Mikhail Gorbachov, to make it plain that Moscow's hesitation over Poland was a turning point in the fortunes of the Soviet empire. Gorbachov came to power already knowing that the Soviet Union had to have a different relationship with its Eastern European satellites. In this, as in many other matters, he was expressing the feelings of a large part of the Soviet intelligentsia for whom the crushing of the Prague Spring had been particularly painful. Gorbachov proposed a policy that was revolutionary: the Eastern Europeans were to be treated as partners. He told them not to expect commands from Moscow but to arrange their affairs as they thought best. Combined with Gorbachov's own re-ordering of the Soviet Union's affairs, this made the Eastern European leaders mightily uncomfortable. They were as used to looking over their shoulder for Moscow's nod as a Catholic is to crossing himself when he enters a church. They had never made a single senior political appointment without clearing it first with the Soviet party. Even Janos Kadar, whose supple and relatively benign (by Eastern European standards) policies seemed closest to Gorbachov's own, was distrustful of the new Soviet General Secretary. Only that man of masks, Wojciech Jaruzelski, kept his nerve and developed a proper relationship with Gorbachov. And only he would survive the revolutionary tide – as the first President of a revived Polish Republic which put the royal crown back on the Polish eagle and struck socialism out of the constitution.

What scared the Eastern European leaders, and what Jaruzelski alone was able to adapt to, was the prospect of a world in which the use of Soviet force, or even the threat of it, was no longer available to back up their regimes. For four decades the people of Eastern Europe had been kept in their place by a simple threat: behave, or the Soviet tanks will come. No big speech by a senior Polish politician was complete without a reference to 'Polish *raison d'état*' – decoded, this meant: we know the situation in the country is bad but there is not much we can do about it without upsetting the Russians, and as we all know the first duty of every good Pole is to help keep them out. After Gorbachov came to power the Eastern European Party bosses would have to prove their manhood by themselves. The question was, did they have the determination and the resources to hold their people in check?

It took time for people to understand what had happened. When the Polish Communists and Solidarity at last agreed in 1989 on a political settlement it was weighted in favour of the Communists. The latter were to be assured a majority in Parliament, the Sejm, because both sides believed it essential – for reasons of that famous Polish *raison d'état* – that the latter keep their hold on power. It needed a humiliating Communist defeat in those seats where the contest was truly open, followed by weeks of nervous negotiation, before Jaruzelski named the Catholic journalist and Solidarity adviser Tadeusz Mazowiecki to lead a coalition government. Warsaw was not struck by Soviet lightning. Perceptive Eastern Europeans could at last be almost sure that Moscow meant what it said: the Communists of Eastern Europe were on their own.

There is no evidence, though, that Gorbachov realised how quickly they would lose power. The Eastern European Communists themselves did not foresee the rapidity of their own decline. It has been a comic feature of all the revolutions that the Communists, at each stage of their descent to powerlessness, deceived themselves into thinking they could break the fall before they reached the bottom. Even Egon Krenz, as implausible a leader for the post-Honecker East Germany as could be imagined, was convinced he could recapture control of events after his old master's departure. It was ridiculous, but it was also understandable. After so many years of unchallenged power it would have been surprising if Krenz and others had behaved any differently. This was the price they paid for exercising power in isolation. A life divided between Party headquarters the size of luxury hotels and private houses that, in East Germany's case, were completely cut off from ordinary people was no preparation for the rough waters of 1989. Neither the Eastern European leaders nor Gorbachov foresaw that the June 1989 elections in Poland would be followed by the rapid unravelling of the Hungarian Communists' attempt at controlled reform; and that by the autumn it would be plain that whoever won Hungary's first free elections in 1990 it was unlikely to be the Hungarian Socialist Party, as the Communists had hopefully re-christened themselves. And then, at a giddy speed no one had imagined, came the German, Czechoslovak and Romanian revolutions. What few people had dared to understand was the extraordinary weakness of the Eastern European regimes. Only perhaps in Czechoslovakia did Vaclav Havel and his colleagues, once the Communist collapse had begun, manoeuvre with the daring of people who had taken proper measure of their opponent's weakness.

Why, after 45 years of unlimited power, were these Communist regimes so weak? By meeting the Soviet requirements for a uniform Communist empire, a supposedly proletarian commonwealth in which class overruled nationality, the Communists of Eastern Europe had lost the chance to speak for their people. Their dilemma was obvious in those moments when, against the odds, a Communist leader who did manage, or seemed to mange, to speak to the national heart. In Poland in 1956 Wladyslaw Gomulka became, briefly, a hero by standing up to the Russians and seeming to promise a Polish road to socialism. In the same year Imre Nagy found himself the popular leader of a Hungarian revolt against Moscow. Twelve years later Alexander Dubcek became the darling of a peaceful, but equally unsuccessful, Czechoslovak attempt to find another, more humane way to socialism.

In truth, all three were questionable national heroes. The Poles soon realised that Gomulka was as much puritan Communist as he was Pole. Nagy and Dubcek lost power too soon to be properly tested, but insofar as they remained Communists their love affair with their people would have come to an end sooner or later. When the Hungarians reburied Nagy with honour in the summer of 1989 the ceremony was puzzlingly ambiguous: were they laying to rest a good Communist, or a good Magyar? It was out of the question for most Hungarians that a man could be both. Nicolai Ceausescu alone among the Eastern European leaders managed over a long period to pose as a national leader. In fact he was only continuing a policy begun by his predecessors to limit Moscow's influence over Romanian economic development, but a challenging anti-Soviet speech during the 1968 Czechoslovak crisis, delivered in the same Bucharest square that 23 years later would see his downfall, gave him popularity. And for some years thereafter his anti-Soviet line continued to win national approval. Later, other Communist leaders would appear who realised that only a new sort of national Communism might save the party. The first successful variety of this hybrid came from outside the bloc in Yugoslavia, where the Serbian Slobodan Milosevic became a national hero by exploiting every possible national grievance from Marshal Tito's discrimination against the Serbs to their diminishing numbers in the southern province of Kosovo. Other national Communists appeared in the Baltic states of the Soviet Union, where resentment against Russian domination was the most powerful force in public life. But this was never a possible choice for the Soviet bloc's Eastern Europeans because by the 1980s the Communists stood accused of far more than destroying national interests and traditions. They were seen to have failed in what they claimed to do best – developing a modern economy and a just society – and they were judged incapable of ever doing better. A break with Moscow there had to be, but it would be made by the Communists' successors.

It is well enough known that not a single Communist Party enjoyed an electoral majority in Eastern Europe at the end of World War II. More often forgotten is that, in spite of their relative initial weakness, the new Communist regimes set out on something like a wave of popularity. There was optimism that the ruins left by the war would quickly be cleared away. The re-building of bombed cities gratified wounded national pride. For many intellectuals, Communism seemed to embody modernity. Communism looked a winner: in the shape of the Soviet army it had defeated Fascism, thus resolving what was seen as the most important political dispute of the age.

For some young Eastern Europeans Communism's idealism, its strong and simple ideas, and not least its hint of power to come, gave it the seductiveness of a cult of personal salvation. At the same time all the countries of Eastern Europe suffered arrests and executions. Labour camps were filled with tens of thousands of those written off as enemies of the bright future. But with the exception of Czechoslovakia, pre-war Eastern Europe, too, had failed to develop democracy, though nowhere had repression been as methodical and widespread as it was to be under the Communists. The pre-war Eastern European societies were often singularly unjust. Their economies for the most part straggled far behind those of Western Europe. The Communists won credit by proposing to break with this bad old history. They promised rapid development and they did indeed bring about a revolutionary social mobility. The physical similarity of so many later Eastern European leaders – usually short men of compact build – was evidence of the way socialism gave opportunities to the brightest sons of predominantly peasant nations. As for the Communists' brutality, it came after years of an extraordinarily brutal war. Sensitivities were numbed, the energy to resist low.

The enthusiasm, such as it was, for the new post-war order did not last long. Stalin in his last mad years saw to that. Hopes of economic development lasted longer and were shared, until remarkably recently, even by some in the West. The Eastern European regimes boasted that they had provided security of life unmatched in the West, and above all they had eradicated unemployment. They were less eager to talk about the productive side of their economies which by the 1980s had not only fallen far behind the West's but also behind some of the emerging countries of the Far East. Starting in the 1970s, Eastern Europe began to pay for a standard of living and a degree of social security that it could not afford by borrowing in the West. The Communists did whatever they could to see that the industrial working class was not disturbed. Rising real food and consumer goods prices were hidden by increasing subsidies. On no account could there by any talk of unemployment. This policy was suicidal, for it either meant going further into debt or consuming resources that should have been reinvested in future development and in dealing with industrial pollution. The result was to be seen in the half-continent's drab and dirty cities, in its deteriorating transport services and in the backwardness of its communications. In Romania, where Ceausescu followed the logic of this evasive policy to its lunatic end, it led to sacrificing the life and health of the population. Why did the Communists stick to such a self-destructive policy? Because, while it was destructive of the country's future, it did not disturb the Party's hold on power, or at least not yet. Far more dangerous, from the Communists' point of view (and Moscow, until 1985, agreed with them entirely), was economic reform, so dangerous in fact that they tried not to use the word in public. The Communist leaders saw correctly that their power depended on maintaining a centrally planned economy where decisions were taken as much for reasons of political advantage as of economic sense. Above all, central planning ensured that the decisions were taken by them, the Communists. Decentralising decision-making by introducing a market – the only reform that was generally seen to make sense – had to bring about a dispersal of power, and put in question the Party's claim to sole authority. It is also true that Eastern European leaders tried not to admit even to themselves the real state of affairs. It was learned after Ceausescu's death that the Romanian grain harvest was only a third of what the government claimed. It seems quite likely that Ceausescu's officials had lied to him, for the system could no longer function if it dealt in truth. There is no doubt that Gunter Mittag, who ran the East German economy, prettified the statistics he showed Erich Honecker. Even in Hungary, a much saner place than East Germany or Romania, most of the Politburo members were not told the truth about the rising foreign debt.

The regimes put their head in the sand and hoped. Only a month before Czechoslovakia's 'velvet revolution', the party leader Milos Jakes was telling foreign visitors that there would be no trouble in his country as long as the workers found goods to buy in the shops and the Party kept control of prices.

By 1989 the threat to Communism in Eastern Europe had swollen like a river fed by many tributary streams. There were the old, undying national grudges against a system imposed by Moscow. *Détente* was making it easier to know more of life in the West, not least because travel restrictions were being eased, and the comparisons grew more and more unfavourable. The economic crisis, though still partly hidden, was making itself felt in unadmitted inflation, shortages and deteriorating social services. Even the trade that bound each country to the Soviet Union was seen, by some, as a handicap. Eastern Europe obtained from Moscow relatively cheap fuel and raw materials but in return much of its industry was locked into the production of goods acceptable to the Soviet market, but unsaleable almost anywhere else in the industrial world. Each country dealt with the political discontent that followed in different ways but none was effective, not least because Gorbachov's own slogans of *glasnost* and *perestroika* could be used as ammunition against the ruling parties. Gorbachov's name, chanted at demonstrations and trials of dissidents, became as subversive as Havel's or Lech Walesa's. In Poland there was a stand-off between the Party and Solidarity: Poles were virtually free except that they could not change the system, an ingenious solution were it not for the dangerous frustration it engendered, particularly among the younger generation. East Germany took the easy way and threw out its troublemakers to the West. The Czechoslovaks were careful to see that the still small number of intellectuals who challenged the system should not develop links with the working class, as had happened in Poland.

These efforts were in vain, and among the first to see it were some of the Communist leaders of Hungary. They were prompted not least by a sense of patriotic alarm, something that was later to echo around all of Eastern Europe. Hungarians, isolated, without a natural ally to call on, could not afford to make mistakes and yet their country was in rapid decline, most obviously compared with Austria to which Hungarians had always felt equal, if not actually superior. Some of the team which replaced Kadar in May 1988 could only see this economic decline. Others believed in a more general decline; that Hungary was in danger of being left behind by the caravan of European civilisation. It was in Hungary that 'Europe' first entered the public language of the Soviet bloc as a codeword signalling a reversal of almost everything that had happened in the previous 40 years. This idea was to appeal to all Eastern Europe for it contained the feeling that great violence had been done to the true nature, or what was now perceived to be the true nature, of its societies. The most radical of Hungary's reform Communists quickly accepted that a market economy could not be separated from political pluralism. Within a year, without being pushed by popular demonstrations, let alone by riots and disorder, they had concluded that the logical end of reform could only be something like bourgeois parliamentary democracy. In this they were at one with all the Hungarian middle class, except perhaps that endangered species, the professors of Marxism-Leninism. And in spite of rumours, there was never much danger of a coup in Budapest by traditional Communists and the security apparatus to restore the old order. The Communist ruling class had lost its nerve for that sort of thing. Instead it consoled itself with the hope that it, too, might find a pleasant enough niche in the new order to come.

The events in Hungary and Poland put the leaders in Prague and East Berlin in an impossible situation. They ruled over populations little inclined to violent revolt or even to sticking their necks out. They also lived quite well, by the modest standards of the bloc. But it was in East Germany and Czechoslovakia that indignation was potentially strongest not only against the cruelty of the system but also its mean-mindedness and ugliness, its dishonesty and plain boredom. It was no coincidence therefore that it was a Czech, the playwright Vaclav Havel, who produced the most eloquent indictment of Communism in Eastern Europe, and the most compelling philosophy of moral and civic resistance to it. The mass escape of East Germans in the summer of 1989 across the newly opened Hungarian border to Austria brought the Germans to a dangerous pitch of discontent. An ill-judged use of force at last pushed them on to the streets in their hundreds of thousands. Something similar happened the following month, November, in Czechoslovakia. In both cases regimes notorious for their reliance on secret policemen gave in to unarmed demonstrators. The men of East Germany's feared ministry of state security, although equipped for all eventualities including nuclear war, could only watch while unarmed men and women laid siege to their headquarters with rings of white candles. In both Czechoslovakia and East Germany a nation walked up to the precipice of civil war and quickly, as though one person, turned back from it. A ruling class recognised that the mandate of heaven had passed from it. These Communists, too, had lost the will to rule.

The violence of the Romanian revolution was the exception because the regime of Nicolai Ceausescu had gone far beyond the grubby authoritarianism into which Communism had degenerated in the rest of Eastern Europe. This peasant's son who became a Communist when still a teenager eventually infested the usual Communist machinery of control like a science fiction monster. But even in Romania most of the men and women who had served Ceausescu quickly changed to the side of the revolution, for the bankruptcy of the old regime was more obvious there than anywhere else. Romania had been forced to live the cruellest parody of the system that was imposed on the Eastern Europeans after 1945. The leadership of a party supposed to represent the interests of the new working class degenerated into the rule of a man whose greed for power was only matched by that of his wife. Over-industrialisation created a working class whose wages could no longer be paid. By the end, the regime was based on nothing but the two unstable pillars of fantasy and violence.

Fantasy and violence in lesser degree marked Communism throughout the Soviet bloc and here lies its tragedy, for both were born out of a certain idealism. The idealism was genuine, but often criminally ill-judged. Call it socialism, call it the age-old longing for social justice and equality in part of the old continent that had seen little of either, it was manipulated from the start by Soviet leaders who had long lost their revolutionary innocence. The result was resistance from all groups or persons of independent inclination: from the

Churches, the peasantry, the intellectuals, and eventually from the working class in whose name the revolutions had been made. After decades of violence – for the most part it needed to be passive, a threat held in reserve – there was little left of those original ideals but fantasy. The Eastern European revolutions of 1989 were a return to reality.

POLAND
Inching towards democracy

14 December 1970	Food riots in Gdansk and other cities lead to removal of Edward Gierek from Party leadership.
14 August 1980	Workers at the Lenin Shipyard in Gdansk form a strike committee.
18 November 1981	Talks on a Front of National Unity begin between the Government and Solidarity.
12–13 December 1981	Martial Law declared; thousands of Solidarity members imprisoned.
30 October 1984	Body of Father Jerzy Popieluszko, Solidarity priest murdered by members of security forces, found.
29 November 1987	National referendum rejects Government reforms.
4 June 1989	First round of first partly free election endorses Solidarity overwhelmingly; Communists crushed.
7 August 1989	Coalition parties change sides; Solidarity offers to form new coalition Government.
24 August 1989	Tadeusz Mazowiecki appointed first non-Communist Prime Minister in the Soviet bloc.
29 December 1989	Sejm eliminates the leading role of the Communist Party in Government.

In August 1989 a gate chained shut for more than 40 years swung open. Without ceremony or apparent emotion, President Wojciech Jaruzelski turned the key and stood aside. He invited Tadeusz Mazowiecki, a lifelong enemy of Soviet Communism, to lead a new coalition Government of the Polish Republic in which Solidarity, not the Polish United Workers' Party, would be the leading force.

It was an event unimaginable through most of the long years of rule by the Communists. Poland's struggle for freedom was a heroic test of endurance, which encompassed the whole of the 1980s. The final year of the decade was an extraordinary one, in which Poland produced the first non-Communist government in the Soviet bloc and led the way for the other people's revolutions that followed, but this historic event was the culmination of a long struggle against increasingly effete Communist rulers who in the end surrendered power not with a bang but a whimper.

In the Sejm – the Polish Parliament – 40 years of docile obedience were quickly forgotten. Down in the hemicycle of seats, under the tall white columns, men and women volubly delivered their thoughts from the rostrum, amendments rose and fell, a Government lost a vote. Deputies laughed, or passed notes, or hurried across the floor to consult one another. Until a few months before, this had been a place where the minister droned through his notes, the deputies yawned, the hands rose in 'total unanimity'.

It was here, in this chamber, that the final act in the Polish revolution took place. Satellite parties that had served as mere appendages to the ruling Communists switched sides, happy at the opportunity to escape from an embrace that they knew would be electoral poison when Poland finally enjoyed a fully free election. Backstairs discussions sealed the deal, and the vote in the Sejm confirmed it. The first non-Communist Government in Eastern Europe took office on a wave of euphoria, tempered only by the knowledge of the appalling challenges that lay ahead.

It had all begun nine years before almost to the day, on 14 August 1980. Changes in the system for selling meat announced the previous month had resulted in price rises of between 90 and 100 percent. Immediately there were strikes, which spread to over 150 plants: along the Baltic coast 500,000 workers downed tools. At the Lenin Shipyard in Gdansk, the management attempted on 14 August to sack a woman crane driver, Anna Walentynowicz, an activist in a fledgling free trade union. The shipyard manager argued with the workers and tried to stop them forming a strike committee. He failed, largely because of the fiery oratory of a shipyard electrician, Lech Walesa, who had been sacked for union activities four years earlier. Walesa persuaded the workers to stay out, and to set up an inter-factory strike committee under his chairmanship. Thus was Solidarity born.

Solidarity was lucky to have found Walesa. For in modern times Poland had produced nothing but a long series of disastrous leaders. The country's geographical position, sandwiched between the Germans and the Russians, must rate as one of the least enviable in the world. But with over 35 million inhabitants, a strong sense of nationhood, a large industrial base, agriculture in private hands, and rich mineral resources, it should not have been impossible for Poland to have become a successful nation within secure borders, given skilled leadership.

The reality had been rather different. Invaded by Hitler, Poland had forced Britain and France finally to face the might of Nazi Germany, but the ultimate Allied victory brought no respite. Of a pre-war population of 20 million, six million were dead, and the nation itself was handed from one tyranny to another when, at Yalta, Roosevelt, Churchill and Stalin redrew the map of post-war Europe. Poland's role was to be a buffer designed to protect the Soviet Union from Germany. At the end of the war Poland's borders had been shifted westward, and its Government fell into Communist hands, with the last word invariably belonging to Moscow.

Other political parties were more or less forcibly amalgamated into the Communist Party, which then renamed itself the Polish United Workers' Party (PUWP). It proved incapable of effective leadership, particularly in economic affairs. There was an abortive attempt at forced industrialisation in the Stalinist period, largely imposed by Moscow. In the 1960s, Wladyslaw Gomulka, leader of the PUWP, allowed the burden of food subsidies to reach gigantic proportions. And when in 1970 the leadership finally braced itself to raise prices, it chose the week before Christmas as its moment, with explosive results. An outbreak of strikes and rioting, especially at Gdansk, resulted in confrontations in which the police opened fire, killing a large number of workers. Throughout the 1970s the Party atrophied under the old-guard leadership of Edward Gierek, and by the end of the decade Poland was suffering the worst economic disaster to hit any European country for over 30 years.

Though it was his boast that he never read books, Lech Walesa was an enlightened man. He had absorbed culture from his mother, who was descended from a landed family whose estate had been divided between hordes of children. Walesa's brilliant off-the-cuff oratory was peppered with references to Polish classical literature. But he also had a cool head, and his shrewd sense of timing was to be a crucial factor over the following decade as Poland stumbled hesitantly towards democracy. As the crisis developed Walesa's popularity spread beyond the Gdansk area. Rapidly Solidarity raised its demands, to include genuinely independent unions, the lifting of press censorship, and the release of dissidents. So widespread did Solidarity's support become that the Government was forced to negotiate. On 30 August 1980 Solidarity won a concession that was historic in a Communist regime. Government negotiators sent from Warsaw agreed to recognise 'independent, self-managing trade unions' with the right to strike, and the concessions were approved at an emergency session of the PUWP Central Committee.

The strikes had destroyed the discredited 10-year-old regime of PUWP leader, Edward Gierek, which collapsed in September. But the Communists faced further challenges as Solidarity made more demands for political freedom and economic reform as the price of industrial peace. The Communist leadership was in an acute dilemma. Faced with growing demands for democracy, even from within its own ranks, the new First Secretary, Stanislaw Kania, dared not move too far for fear of meeting the same fate as Alexander Dubcek in Czechoslovakia in 1968. On the other hand, if the Party failed to reform itself it risked further antagonising the Polish people and losing control completely.

The danger of a Soviet invasion was not to be ignored. Since the end of World War II the Soviet Union's response to protest in Eastern Europe had been brutal repression. There were 40 Soviet divisions around Poland's borders, and the Soviet, East German and Czechoslovak media were united in their condemnation of Solidarity. The political danger to Poland's Communist neighbours was that the ideas emanating from Gdansk could prove highly infectious. The military risk was that the Soviet Union's lines of communication to East Germany would be severed in Poland. On 5 December 1980 an unexpected Warsaw Pact summit in Moscow declared Warsaw's problems to be a matter for the Socialist community as a whole, an alarming hint of what might follow.

To assuage Moscow's fears, General Jaruzelski, the Defence Minister, was appointed Prime Minister in February 1981. A Soviet-trained general, he was regarded as relatively moderate since on three previous occasions, in 1970, 1976 and 1980, he had refused to let the Polish army be used against strikers. At first it was not clear whether this would be enough to reassure the Russians. Between February and October, large-scale Soviet exercises involving 200,000 troops were held close to the Polish border. In a letter to the Polish Central Committee which began 'Dear Comrades', the Kremlin intimated that the Polish leadership no longer held its confidence. Fierce criticism of 'revisionism' continued unabated in the Soviet press.

With more strikes threatened, Solidarity's leaders realised they could no longer control the wave of militancy they had unleashed. The Government was in danger of losing control, even of its own supporters. A huge rift had opened up between the Communist leadership and the rank and file, many of whom were willing to go on strike. Walesa toured the country urging restraint and calm, and when Jaruzelski appealed to the nation for a 90-day moratorium on strikes the Solidarity leadership agreed. In the end Moscow's tanks did not move on Poland. The Kremlin may have been deterred by the prospect of Western outrage, or may have believed that the Polish Communist Party could retain its grip. Moscow's decision to hold its hand allowed the tiny flame of democracy that had been lit at Gdansk to continue to burn.

In July Poland passed another milestone by holding a Party Congress which was not, for once, a rubber stamp. Meeting against a background of growing political crisis, an Emergency Congress of the PUWP in Warsaw's Stalinist-Gothic Palace of Culture voted a number of Solidarity members on to its Central Committee and rejected seven of the outgoing 11-member Politburo. In July the Government introduced economic reforms to decentralise decision-making and allow market mechanisms to work. But without political solutions confrontation with Solidarity, now a major national move-ment with 10 million members, was unavoidable. In September 1981 at its first national congress in Gdansk, Solidarity called for sweeping reforms, including workers' control, union access to the mass media, and open elections to local councils and to the Sejm to break the regime's monopoly of candidates, who all had to be nominated through the 'Front of National Unity'. Solidarity leaders were con-vinced that without valid political institutions enjoying democratic legitimacy, there was no chance of carrying through the great economic reforms which the Government, the trade unions and the population all agreed had to take place.

During the autumn the hope of a deal between Solidarity and the Government stayed alive, if only just. After refusing Solidarity's demands for workers' self-management and insisting that it would defend to the end the principle of the *nomenklatura* (the right to nominate candidates to all leading posts in Polish institutions) the wind appeared to change. Stefan Olszowski, the toughest member of the Politburo, suggested on TV that the Catholic Church and Solidarity might join the Front of National Unity through which the Party and its satellites dominated elections. As Poland's appalling economic crisis continued to worsen, the Party's Central Committee in desperation replaced Stanislaw Kania as First Secretary with General Jaruzelski, who was already Prime Minister and Minister of Defence. Though the Party had a 'guiding role' it appeared to realise that it had to take other centres of power into account, principally the independent farmers and industrial unions and the Catholic Church under its new and as yet untried Primate, Archbishop Jozef Glemp. There had already been talk of some kind of coalition of Government,

Church and Solidarity. Walesa himself was in a conciliatory mood. 'We do not want to overthrow the power of the State', he said. 'Let the Government govern the country and we will govern ourselves in the factories.'

On 4 November Walesa met Jaruzelski and Archbishop Glemp, and on 18 November Solidarity and the Government opened talks on the formation of a 'Front of National Unity'. The talks went badly. By December, Solidarity and Jaruzelski's Government were on a collision course. The Government intended to put through the Sejm a package of emergency laws to allow it to ban strikes, prohibit meetings, and use courts martial for some civilian offences. Solidarity threatened a one-day national strike, to be followed by an unlimited General Strike, if the measures were put into force. Threatened with industrial anarchy, Jaruzelski claimed there was a plot to overthrow the socialist state. During the night of 12 December 1981, the army seized power from the Communist Party and imposed martial law in the name of 'order and discipline'. Tens of thousands of Solidarity members were arrested, and Jaruzelski's decrees banned almost every sort of social activity beyond going to work, standing in a queue, or praying. A so-called Military Council of National Salvation was formed.

What followed was the nadir of Solidarity's fortunes, a dark night of suppression and imprisonment. The opposition was ruthlessly harried and all anti-Government demonstrations and expressions of opinion stifled. There were purges of academics, journalists and workers. Finally on 9 October 1982 Solidarity was banned and the Sejm created new official unions. The right to strike was permitted as a last resort, but not on political issues.

Martial law produced a howl of rage from outside the country. The rise of Solidarity had been followed with hope by many who saw it as the first real crack in the Communist monolith. The West's reaction was to freeze export credits to Poland and to refuse to reschedule Poland's debts. It demanded an end to martial law and internment, and a resumption of dialogue with the Church and the independent unions. The Council of Bishops demanded freedom for those interned, free trade unions and the restoration of Solidarity.

Yet, significantly, Jaruzelski did not follow through with the conventional Communist pattern of 'normalisation' which usually follows an upheaval. Instead of the years of undifferentiated terror against most of the population which applied in Hungary after 1956 and in Czechoslovakia after 1968, Jaruzelski's regime adopted a selective approach, slackening the pressure against the majority while intensifying it against active or outspoken opponents of the regime.

The Church's role during this period was crucial. With an inborn dislike of strife and a prudent eye to its own position, the Church played a moderating role in the hope of extracting more Government concessions. The Church's caution against street protests paid dividends. In November it was announced that the Pope would visit Poland the following June. What was not announced was that the visit, which had been postponed, was on conditions laid down by the Vatican: the release of internees, the lifting of martial law, an amnesty and genuinely independent trade unions. Solidarity accepted a blueprint drawn up by the Church in consultation with the Pope for dialogue between rulers and ruled, which was intended to lead to pluralism and popular participation within the existing system, and the cancellation of martial law.

On 12 November Walesa was released. During his imprisonment the movement had survived underground, while he had continued to communicate with his followers through smuggled messages. In the outside world, his reputation had never stood higher, and in 1983 he was awarded the Nobel Peace Prize, though he was not allowed to leave Poland to collect it.

The man who emerged from jail after 11 months was without any doubt the unofficial leader of the opposition in Poland. His hold over his fellow workers came in the first place from his oratory. Before the Gdansk strike on August 1980, the small committee that prepared it – the Free Trade Union of the Coast, as it was called – did not think too highly of him. He niggled about details, while the intellectuals wanted to discuss vast ideas. It was only when he was pulled over the shipyard fence and began to speak that his talents emerged.

In jail he was isolated, cut off from the conversation he adores, and provided with enormous meals, no exercise and all the cigarettes he wanted. He survived this poisonous mixture and emerged fatter, paler and a little greyer. He went back to Gdansk, to a dreary high-rise shared with his wife Danuta and their eight children, and was eventually allowed back to work as an electrician at the shipyard. He went into retreat; but it was the retreat of the leader who confidently expects to be summoned once more. It was the obscurity of the private citizen to whose door the world beats a path.

Walesa is a consummate politician, a manipulator who can make a crowd change its mind three times in 10 minutes. He greatly enjoyed the process of negotiation – 'Pole must talk things out with Pole', he used to declare. He is crafty, as his long nose and foxy, russet eyes suggest. But he is also tough, able to resist not only the pressures of the Party, but the more insidious damage that can come with fame. After the strike in 1980 succeeded and Solidarity emerged, he might have been swallowed up by the blaze of fawning publicity, the mouth-watering offers, the flattery from the West and even from those who had been pursuing him in Poland for the previous 10 years. But he survived as his own man, a Polish original.

For most of the 1980s, Walesa waited, his message the same. 'You will have to talk to us again. Without the authentic public consent which only Solidarity can deliver, the economic reform programme can never succeed.' The claim was not immodest, though Walesa is not a particularly modest man. It was the simple truth.

He emerged from prison with his colleagues from Solidarity to a surprising discovery – Poland was not a political wasteland. In addition to the Solidarity underground network there were numerous new groupings producing an extraordinary range of samizdat newspapers, journals and books. Far from being snuffed out, the opposition to Communist rule had been broadened and strengthened.

On 30 December martial law was provisionally lifted, though some 5000 people remained in prison and workers were still forbidden to change jobs without permission. In January 1983 the Government proceeded with its plans to form 2500 legally registered workplace-based unions and ban political strikes. At the same time, Jaruzelski attempted to implement a number of reforms to revive the flagging economy, including the relatively bold step of allowing greater autonomy for factories. But absenteeism remained rife and productivity continued to fall. The Communist Party itself sank into torpor, shedding 1.5 million of its three million members. Faced with apathy on all sides, Jaruzelski began to drop the harshest provisions of his rule and to consult more closely with the Church and with Cardinal Glemp. By July 1983 Jaruzelski felt sufficiently confident that calm had been restored to bring martial law to an end. The Russians had apparently accepted him as an upholder of the *status quo*, and the threat of Soviet military intervention had receded.

In October 1984, international protests erupted once more when the mutilated body of Father Popieluszko, a priest who had become legendary for highly patriotic sermons supporting Solidarity, was found in the river Vistula. Over 250,000 attended his funeral. Jaruzelski claimed that the Government bore no responsibility for the abduction and murder of the priest, and appealed for the Pope's help in maintaining calm. He also removed political control of the Interior Ministry from the Politburo. The following February, four secret police officers were sentenced to 14–25 years' imprisonment for the murder.

By December 1985 the Party had degenerated into a feeble instrument of Government. While the top officials were often hardline, the rank and file lacked zeal. The underground magazine, *Przeglady*, published figures from a confidential official poll which showed that ordinary Party members had much the same views as other Poles. A large proportion of them seemed to read the underground press. Only 38 percent had any confidence in their own

Central Committee. A quarter were believing and practising Catholics, while another 49 percent believed, but went to Mass seldom or never.

Unsurprisingly, the great economic reform projects came to a halt in a mire of vested interests. The Party had neither the power nor the imagination to get things moving again. Poland drifted slowly towards an even graver economic crisis, crippled by debt, unable to modernise its industry, relying on the luck of good harvests and the traditional export of coal.

The arrival on the international scene of Mikhail Gorbachov transformed the situation by making reform a legitimate objective for both sides. The Polish Government and the opposition could both legitimately claim to be working in the spirit of *glasnost* and *perestroika*. The Communists, wishing to remain in power by adapting to change, argued that their moves towards a freer market economy and more democracy were in line with the latest Soviet thinking. For its part, Solidarity knew that Gorbachov's policies gave them greater space to breath, since he was calling for changes they had been advocating for years. But the Polish opposition would have remained strong even if Gorbachov had not come to power. The roots of the unrest in Poland lay not in events in the Soviet Union, but in the Church, the underground press, political clubs and discussion groups. Most of the opposition leaders released from jail had simply gone back to doing what they had been doing before they were sent there, such as organising, writing, or printing underground newspapers.

Jaruzelski tried to devolve economic and political power, to tempt non-Party people and the moderate opposition into sharing responsibility for society with his Government. On the surface there was movement, even progress. The US dropped its sanctions against Poland. The amnesty for political prisoners was welcomed, and a few independent figures who were Solidarity supporters consented to join a new 'consultative council' advising the supreme Council of State. The Minister of Culture, Aleksander Krawczuk, spoke in tolerant tones of Poland's large underground publishing industry, and tried to build bridges between the Union of Writers and former members who had dominated it in the Solidarity period before they were expelled. Yet most people experienced the economic reforms only as steep price rises, while the old industrial cartels remained fossilised. Even the new trade unions formed to replace Solidarity were asserting that 40 percent of the population lived below the 'social minimum'.

Brief sparks of protest kept weakening the Government's resolve to act. In March 1987, for example, the price of sour cream was sharply raised in the coalfields. Several mines stopped work and by evening the shop price was back to where it started. 'Nothing ever happens', one politician said. 'You make a proposal, then the trade unions oppose it, the local authorities and the security police report discontent, and it's withdrawn.' The Government had lost all its energy, another senior figure said. 'It used up all its strength and imagination in the battle against Solidarity in 1981–82.'

Yet still Poland continued to show that it was not a typical Soviet-bloc state, producing democratic initiatives remarkable by the normal standards of Eastern Europe, though not always with the results the authorities intended. In November 1987 General Jaruzelski decided to hold a referendum to win national support for a programme of radical reform, which included price rises. The voters were asked two questions: Did they want a painful programme of economic reform? And did they want various vaguely formulated democratic reforms? It was a highly risky undertaking, and as it turned out, a spectacular own goal by Jaruzelski. The turnout was 67 percent. Of those who voted, 66 percent said Yes to the economic reforms and 69 percent to the democratic reforms. Yet it was still a defeat for the Government. For it had added a special provision: if less than 51 percent of the registered electorate voted Yes, then the proposals would be considered rejected. This was a suicidal amendment, for it was almost inevitable that between them, the abstainers and the no-voters would constitute a majority. Adding in the abstentions reduced the proportion of Polish electors voting Yes to 44 and 46 percent. The reason for such imprudence was that the Polish Government wanted to look as democratic as Solidarity, which had introduced utopian electoral rules governing its own affairs. The West had a hearty laugh at the general's discomfiture, yet it was another first for Poland, the first electoral consultation in the Soviet half of Europe since 1945 in which the voting was free and fair and the results not faked. Putting a brave face on the result, Jaruzelski said that the radical economic reforms and limited political democratisation would go ahead anyway.

By 1988 Poland's economy was disappearing into a black hole. There were first the colossal foreign debts, brought about chiefly by the need to buy off consumer and labour unrest during the 1980s. Then, in spite of the economic reform programme, there was stagnation, falling living standards and the possibility of another full-blown economic collapse leading to a political explosion. Price inflation and shortages, the decay of welfare, especially the health services, and the decline of the industrial system which could not replace machinery because of the shortage of foreign exchange, all formed a threatening prospect. A poll showed that between 20 and 30 percent of Poles would like to emigrate to the West.

In the spring of 1988 a wave of strikes over wage restraint and price rises spread across the country. The Gdansk shipyard, birthplace of

Solidarity, and the steel works of Nowa Huta were occupied by strikers. Solidarity banners were raised, the yard gates festooned with flowers and pictures of the Pope, and Walesa was back in action. Transport workers joined in. In August more price rises triggered off another massive surge of strikes. One of the main demands was the re-legalisation of Solidarity and the reinstatement of Walesa. The sheer scale and organisation of the strikes caught the Government completely off balance. Walesa demanded talks with the Government, and the Government conceded.

Gradually, as Poland's crisis deepened, the ruling Communists had thrown away one dogma after another. Overboard had gone central planning, the fetish of nationalised property, the principle of thought control and the power of the secret police. But one principle remained intact; that Communist Parties, once in power, never relinquish it. Now even that was to fall. Since the previous August, Walesa had been putting forward ambitious demands for round table meetings with the Government to draw up the shape of a new transitional Polish constitution. The Government had repeatedly refused. There was opposition to the idea from within Solidarity itself, especially from the radical Solidarity Working Group, which repeatedly warned Walesa against 'playing political games' with the authorities. At Solidarity meetings they even greeted him with shouts of 'Traitor' and 'no talks with murderers'.

But the decision to close the Lenin Shipyard, in line with the Government's new market-oriented philosophy, had been one more piece of evidence to Walesa that problems could no longer be solved by strikes. The Solidarity mainstream decided it had to cooperate with the Government. 'We are in the same country. Therefore we are in the same camp', Walesa said with weary resignation.

Jaruzelski too had come to realise that there was no alternative. The political logjam began to move. In addition to Jaruzelski himself, there were two other prime movers. One was the Prime Minister, Mieczyslaw Rakowski, who risked a split in the Party by arguing for a candid admission that martial law had failed, and that there had to be a fresh start. The other was the Interior Minister and chief of the secret police, General Czeslaw Kiszczak. He had established a curious relationship with the opposition, despite being their sworn enemy. He maintained contacts with them, and became one of the most important sponsors of the round table negotiations. As the idea of negotations took root, Walesa persuaded the militants to call off strikes so that Solidarity could offer 'responsible negotiations', and in December the Government finally accepted the offer of round table talks. At 3 am on 18 January, after an acrimonious session during which Jaruzelski was attacked by hardline critics, the Central Committee approved proposals to allow an expansion of political and trade union activity. The Party formally declared its readiness to lift the 1982 ban on trade unions. The round table discussions which involved the Government, Solidarity and the Roman Catholic Church were to have immense consequences for Poland's future. They started on 5 February, and on 5 April a historic agreement was finally signed, one which was to transform the political landscape. It was a classic compromise. In a number of far-reaching concessions the authorities agreed to legalise Solidarity and recognise the right to strike. A private farmer's union, Rural Solidarity, was also to be set up. The office of President was to be created. Elections were to be held on 4 June, and there was to be a new upper house, the Senate, which was to be freely elected. At the same time there would be elections to the main parliament, the Sejm, but with only one-third of the seats open to contest by the opposition. The remaining seats would be filled by the Communists and their allies, who would thereby be guaranteed a 65 percent majority. In addition, the voters were to be asked to endorse a special 'National List' of 35 leading Communists and Communist supporters, most of whom had played key roles at the round table. The package was a temporary solution. In effect, Solidarity was accepting the job of propping up a dilapidated house on the verge of collapse so that a thorough reconstruction could take place later, on the basis of plans not yet agreed.

The first Polish election campaign for more than 60 years in which freely nominated candidates were allowed to participate began on 1 May. Walesa launched Solidarity's election campaign at a rally of 7000 supporters in Gdansk. Clambering on to a wooden barrel outside St Brygid's Church where the union had been created in 1980, he shouted: 'If we all care for Poland, then go together to the polls and vote. We like to win and I like to win, so we will win a better Poland.' The opposition election posters of Gary Cooper wearing a Solidarity badge suggested that the election represented a kind of high noon for Poland, yet as far as real power was concerned it was more like a pistol duel with dummy bullets. Since the Polish United Workers' Party and its coalition were assured of 65 percent of Sejm seats, the real question as to who was to govern Poland was postponed. 'It is impossible to move at one jump from an authoritarian system to democracy', insisted Solidarity's Professor Bronislaw Geremek.

Nevertheless, for the first time in the Soviet bloc there was to be genuine electoral choice. The fight was for the 'opposition' 35 percent of seats, where anyone who could raise 3000 signatures could stand. In practice, Solidarity found itself confronted by so-called 'independents'. These were essentially members of the *nomenklatura*, holders of jobs to which they had been appointed by the Party. But all were at pains to avoid ever describing themselves as Communists, knowing that the designation would be fatal to their chances. In fact, many were directors of enterprises, and in the campaign they defended their own values, those of thrusting, self-reliant ambition. On posters they postively glistened with success. Men like Director Tuderek of Budimex, the state construction firm or Dominyk Jastrzebski, Minister of Foreign Trade, talked unadulterated Thatcherism. Solidarity too stood for a market economy, freed from state direction, but with qualifications. It was Solidarity, not the *nomenklatura*, which wanted to soften the impact of market forces by linking wages to prices in times of raging inflation and by pressing for genuine worker self-government in the factories and workplaces.

But all the signs were that the voters were not interested in such niceties. The electorate was clearly not going to waste its first chance in years to comment on the regime that had brought Poland to such a disaster by voting in its nominees.

There was a sense of unreality about the campaign. Men and women who had been chased, harrassed, beaten and locked up for more than a decade were now running as senators and deputies, their faces on huge posters rather than on snapshots pinned to 'wanted' lists. There was unreality, too, in the apparent belief of the Communists and their satellite partners in the ruling coalition that they could fight a real election as though they were a real political party rather than a trade union of the privileged and powerful. They presented themselves as the party of law, order and calm, and one Central Committee Secretary predicted that Solidarity would fail to win half of the seats it was allowed to contest for the Sejm, and that the Government would win a small majority in the Senate.

The coalition seemed blind to the thousands of young Solidarity election workers out in the streets campaigning, and to the overwhelming number of people signing nomination forms for Solidarity candidates. Most Solidarity candidates got 10,000 signatures, and in some Warsaw constituencies up to 80,000. At Poznan, Solidarity's two candidates for the Senate received a record 90,000 signatures, 10 percent of the whole electorate, half of them collected outside churches after Sunday Mass. Both Solidarity candidates had been interned during the martial law period. 'They can dress up sufferers almost as saints', sighed one industrial boss 'and what Pole can resist that?' By contrast, when Communist leaders invited electors to meetings and even enticed them with offers of food and drinks, nobody turned up.

The election was fought reasonably fairly and certainly with decorum, though Solidarity accused the Government of scheduling its TV broadcasts late at night. A brilliant and sophisticated campaign by

Solidarity and the full resources of the Roman Catholic Church ensured that while many voters did not know who to vote for on the complicated ballot papers, they knew which names to cross out. On election day Solidarity set up information booths outside all 20,000 polling stations around the country. All were equipped with crib sheets to help voters cope with the lists. In Warsaw the crib sheets actually showed mock ballot papers, filled in to indicate which names to cross out. Inside the polling station some voters made no attempt to hide these useful guides.

The electorate's verdict was devastating, a massive thumbs down to the Communists and their supporters. Even an attempt by Solidarity, by now alarmed at the possibility of anarchy, to persuade its supporters to leave the names of champions of reform on the National List was to no avail. One stipulation of the round table agreement had been that National List candidates had to receive more than 50 percent of the votes to be elected. Only two of the 35 candidates on the list succeeded. One of them was Mikolaj Kozaliewicz, a Peasant Party member who had gained a reputation for independence, the other Adam Zielinski, a Communist administrative law judge who may have survived because his name was at the bottom of the list where it was overlooked by voters crossing off the names of official candidates.

Virtually the entire Communist leadership was eliminated. Among them were Prime Minister Mieczyslaw Rakowski, who announced he would not seek a seat in the next Parliament, and Interior Minister General Kiszczak, who had helped create the round table. Another casualty was Jerzy Urban, the well known but little loved former Government spokesman, scourge of Solidarity and of foreign journalists. Urban, who had been responsible for the highly partisan television coverage of the campaign, was roundly defeated by his Solidarity opponent, Andrezej Lapiacki, a well known actor, who gained around 80 percent of the vote.

Solidarity swept all before it. It won 82 of the 100 Senate seats on the first ballot, and increased its total to 99 out of 100 on the second ballot two weeks later. It won all 161 seats allocated to the opposition in the Sejm. The only non-Solidarity winner in the Senate was Henryk Soklosa, who could be said to be a special case. An ex-Communist turned millionaire entrepreneur, he stood as an independent and claimed to have spent £100,000 on his campaign.

The turn-out in the second round on 19 June was another withering comment on the regime by the voters. Most of the remaining contests were between Communists of different hues in seats where no candidate had succeeded in gaining the decisive 50 percent of the votes in the first round. Only a miserable 25 percent bothered to vote in these so called 'red elections'. In some constituencies, Solidarity recommended a vote for the more reform-minded of the Communists, and all these won easily. In some constituencies where Solidarity had expressed no preference, only six percent voted. The result left the country without effective government. Solidarity did not have a majority. The Communists, with their 65 percent of the seat given to them uncontested, had no popular support. The election result was not really what Solidarity wanted either, for it was not prepared for power. It had never wished to seize power, and had become convinced reluctantly of the need to share it in order to achieve reform only after several years of rudderless government. It was not even a political party. The trade union which owned the name had endorsed a much broader 'Solidarity' electoral list, including Catholic activists, private business people and others as candidates. Solidarity was a house divided against itself. It could not be a trade union and a government since in troubled times the two would be in natural opposition to each other. Its trade union wing was concerned mainly with maintaining workers' rights and living standards, while its political wing supported tough reforms, which involved closing factories and freezing incomes.

The movement was rent by deep divisions. There were those who sought to change the system from within, such as Walesa himself, while others believed the entire structure had to be blown to bits. There were Roman Catholic conservatives on the watch for godless liberalism. Activists in the provinces distrusted Warsaw, while farmers did not always see eye to eye with workers, and both bore grudges against Walesa's intellectual advisers.

Meanwhile, the Communist infrastructure remained in place. Despite the western-style political confrontations that emerged in the newly elected Parliament, Poland was effectively under the control of the 17-member Politburo, whose members had been elected by the Central Committee. But power was inexorably slipping away from the Communists. The Party's parliamentary group voted to support the creation of a new Government whose members would be subject to the discipline only of Parliament. In a remarkable resolution passed in August, Parliament voted by 335 votes to one, with nine abstentions, to condemn the 1968 Soviet-led invasion of Czechoslovakia. The resolution said that the intervention had 'breached the inalienable right of every nation to self-determination and its natural desire for democracy, freedom and respect for human rights'.

Growing defections among the PUWP's smaller party allies, who foresaw political oblivion if they remained tainted with the Communist label, even put in doubt the election of a Communist as President. The opposition's strategy was to have Jaruzelski elected President as a guarantee to the Russians that Poland would stay in the Warsaw Pact. Reluctantly Jaruzelski ran for the post and on 19 July was elected by a single vote, with the tacit support of the Solidarity leadership. Jaruzelski's first step was to try to form a Communist-led Government. On 25 July he invited Solidarity to be the junior partner in a coalition under the Communists, but Walesa, biding his time skilfully, refused. On 31 July Rakowski, his leadership paralysed by the election result, stepped down after 10 months as Prime Minister and became Communist Party leader. One of his last acts was to scrap food subsidies, almost without warning, in a bid to force agriculture to switch to Western methods. The consequence was soaring food prices, as farmers refused to sell any more meat to the state purchasing monopoly. The new prices were the equivalent of £20 for a pound of pork chops, £40 for a pound of sirloin. The result was round after round of warning strikes, mostly one-hour affairs. At first they were about pay and local injusticies. Then inevitably they became political.

On 2 August, General Kiszczak was appointed Prime Minister. But the sight of the same old faces exchanging places with one another at the top provoked real desperation. The strikers began to demand a Solidarity Government. A political general strike seemed just round the corner, and beyond that, mass convulsions out of anybody's control.

The situation was dramatically resolved by Walesa on 7 August. From his flat in Gdansk, away from all his advisers, he phoned the Polish news agency with a statement inviting the two partners of the PUWP Party, the Peasants and Democratic Parties, to break with their four decades of support for the Communists and ally themselves with Solidarity to form a Government. Together they would control 55 percent of the votes. The earlier hostility of the two minority party leaders, Roman Malinowski, the Peasants Party leader, and Jerzy Joswiak, the Democratic leader, had already begun to crumble as the result of pressure from their parliamentary group. At a meeting on 16 August they gratefully agreed.

That night the Solidarity parliamentarians were suddenly invited to vote for a new coalition. The satellite parties appeared in the chamber to offer their loyalty, soon followed by the apparition of Walesa himself from Gdansk. Their combined votes carried the day. Most deputies thought they were in fact voting in Walesa as Prime Minister. But afterwards, the vote won, he told the press that he did not want to be Prime Minister after all. By then, nobody cared. The sense of challenge was surging through Solidarity's veins, though the parliamentarians had done little more than put their stamp on a deal already signed and sealed.

The following day Walesa and the heads of the two minority parties met Jaruzelski. Much depended on the President's reaction. He sought first to establish that there was sufficient common ground between the three parties, and if there were adequate guarantees for the nation's defence and its internal security. Earlier Jaruzelski had declared that the anxiety of Poland's Warsaw Pact neighbours was the main obstacle to a Solidarity-led Government. But Walesa had already moved to forestall this objection. At the price of offending many Solidarity members, he declared that Poland should remain a member of the Warsaw Pact, and that a Solidarity-led coalition should contain Communists as Ministers of Defence and of the Interior. 'Poland cannot forget where it is situated, to whom it has obligations. You know we are in the Warsaw Pact. That cannot be changed', he said.

It was enough for Jaruzelski. He was ready to give his approval to the first non-Communist Government in Eastern Europe since World War II. Walesa was proposed as leader of a coalition Government, but he refused. He told Polish radio that he would lead the efforts to form Solidarity Government, but would not accept the nomination to be Prime Minister.

Shyness, piety, and possibly a distrust of all power played a part in this reluctance. He regarded his role as that of guide and counsellor to the union, outside Parliament. Walesa, the shipyard electrician who had become the most powerful man in Poland, said he preferred to remain a worker, 'a man of the people. I stay with the masses. I am one of them.' But there was also an element of cool calculation in his decision, for whoever took over would be able to offer the Polish people no prospect other than blood, sweat and tears.

There were three candidates for the premiership, all from Solidarity: the leader of the parliamentary faction of the opposition, Professor Bronislaw Geremek, a well known mediaeval historian, Jacek Kuron, an opposition activist for 20 years who had spent nine years in prison and was a popular politician, and Tadeusz Mazowiecki, editor of *Solidarity Weekly*.

Many expected that Geremek would be selected. Some of the best known Solidarity activists favoured his candidacy. He was telegenic: with his beard and pipe, he could have passed for a ship's captain. But his career was witness to the shifting balance of forces in the country. He had once been a Communist, having left the Party in 1968. The Church and the right-wing of Solidarity therefore harboured suspicions.

It was up to Jaruzelski to present his choice to the Sejm. In practice, both Geremek and Kuron left the way clear for Mazowiecki, a 62-year-old widower with three children, who was the candidate most acceptable to Jaruzelski because his opposition to Communist rule in previous years had been moderately expressed. A lay Roman Catholic intellectual, he was a co-founder of a scholarly, Church-affiliated monthly called *Wiez*, which he had edited between 1958 and 1981. He had been a controversial and outspoken parliamentary deputy representing the Znak group of lay Catholics between 1961 and 1971, and in the late 1970s he founded a revolutionary system of alternative education called the 'Flying University'. Leading teachers and university lecturers would give clandestine lessons in private flats to students eager to get away from politically approved lessons. At the time of the founding of Solidarity, he became one of Walesa's closest advisers. His key role had been to marshal Warsaw intellectual support for the striking shipyard workers on the Baltic. In 1981 he became editor-in-chief of Solidarity's weekly newspaper, *Tygodnik Solidarnosc*, until it was suppressed by the martial law decrees in December, and he spent a year in jail. With Geremek he had coordinated the negotiations for the opposition during round table talks.

The official termination of one-party rule came finally at 1.08 pm 24 August when Mazowiecki was elected as the first non-Communist Prime Minister in the history of the Soviet bloc. It was an emotional occasion in Parliament. As Mazowiecki's name was announced, every member rose. Mazowiecki crossed behind the Speaker's chair and shook hands with the entire former Communist Cabinet. Then he turned to be embraced and kissed on both cheeks first by Geremek as Solidary's parliamentary leader, and then by Solidarity's top activists and by the leaders of the United Peasants Party and Democratic Party. Watching on television at his home in Gdansk, Walesa wiped tears from his eyes.

There were 378 votes in favour, 41 Communist abstentions, and four votes against. Even on the Communist benches there was laughter and finger-pointing at the four die-hards who refused to vote for Mazowiecki. But the prevailing sentiment was awe, and some disbelief, especially among the many deputies who had spent years behind bars. Geremek captured the spirit of the occasion best: 'For the first time in 45 years, a Polish Government is to be formed, on Polish soil, by non-Communist forces', he said. 'The monopoly of the party which ruled Poland against the will of the people has been broken.'

The Parliament also formally accepted the resignation of General Kiszczak, the powerless Prime Minister of only a few weeks standing, who had brought in martial law as Interior Minister. So magnanimous was the mood that he too was thanked and applauded. Mazowiecki was promised support by a senior Communist Party leader, Mr Marek Krol, who told journalists: 'The Communist Party parliamentary caucus will do everything so that this Government is successful.'

Mazowiecki received a congratulatory message from the Soviet Union, and one of his first acts was to telephone the Vatican and talk to the Pope.

On 12 September the Sejm voted by 402–0 with 13 abstentions for the first Cabinet free from Communist domination. When the vote was announced Mazowiecki gave a V for victory sign, and pronounced the 40 years of Communist rule formally over. Earlier in the proceedings, however, the fragility of the Cabinet constructed by Mazowiecki was suggested when the Prime Minister had to break off his speech because of a dizzy spell. He returned after 45 minutes to a standing ovation to state: 'I am sorry, but this is the result of several weeks of too intensive work. I've reached the same condition as the Polish economy. But I will have to get over it, and so will the economy.'

The new Cabinet was made up of 11 Solidarity ministers, four Communists, four Peasant Party and three Democratic Party ministers. Its members were a ragout of extremely varied ingredients. Those who had expected Mazowiecki to appoint a left-leaning, trade union-dominated Cabinet were in for a surprise. The new Cabinet showed most strikingly the contrasting flavours of Solidarity itself.

While the outside world had got used to thinking of Solidarity as a left-of-centre movement, the choice of ministers reflected the philosophy of economic liberalism, combined with recognition of harsh political necessities. Mazowiecki gave the economic ministries to three liberal Solidarity economists who were committed to the free market. The Finance Minister was 42-year-old Leszek Balcerowicz, a former Communist who left the Party in 1981, and became a fervent advocate of the 'marketisation' of the Polish economy. The Industry Minister was 41-year-old Tadceucz Syryjcfzyk, an engineer, private entrepreneur, and former regional Solidarity leader who believed in the need for changes in the ownership system, more private industry and free trade with the West. Also included were Solidarity leaders from Catholic and conservative circles, and one name that harked back to the pre-war Polish right-wing, that of Professor Krzysztof Skubiszewski, the new Foreign Minister, who had stood as an Independent.

But the Communists still retained four key ministries – Defence, the Interior, Transport and Foreign Trade. The four Communists included the politically experienced General Kiszczak, who became Interior Minister and one of four Deputy Prime Ministers. The Communists also continued to control the state bureaucracy and the diplomatic corps, all of which was expected to restrict the new Prime Minister's room for manoeuvre.

Mazowiecki was the first Polish Prime Minister since the war to invoke God's aid for his task. 'Poles must open a new chapter in their history', he said. 'I believe God will help us to take this huge step on the road ahead.' Before the deputies arrived for the session he had entered the hall and sat alone, apparently praying, in the empty benches reserved for the Government.

Across the country the Solidarity-led Government began removing PUWP members from their guaranteed and privileged positions in industry. It cut off all official subsidies to the PUWP, a severe blow for the Party which could cover only a fraction of its costs from membership fees. Most of their money came from their control of the press consortium, which printed and distributed all officially sponsored newspapers, a monopoly that was swiftly broken up. The Treasury had also paid subsidies to the Communists and granted low-interest loans. All this too was cut off from 1 January 1990.

Forced to make money to survive, the Communists had to use their only assets, their barrack-like headquarters in every provincial city and their fleets of black Volga limousines. The port of Szczecin seized the initiative and decided to open a driving school, using its official Party cars. Buses that formerly ferried Party workers on weekend outings were rented out to tourist companies. Half of the Party headquarters was let. In Lodz the Party car fleet became Rent-a-Limousine, complete with Communist chauffeur, a service that proved popular with organisers of funerals. A hotel previously reserved for Communist dignitaries was opened to the public. Most humiliating of all, the ideological training centre was turned into a nightclub. Elsewhere Party offices were transformed into management training centres, and conference halls which had once been filled with applauding Party delegates were rented out as discotheques. In Warsaw there were plans to rent out part of the Party secretariat to a bank and to set up a commercial art gallery in the other part.

On 29 December the Sejm passed a series of constitutional amendments sweeping away the vestiges of Stalinism. It formally removed the Party's leading role in the Government, restored the nation's pre-war name, the Republic of Poland, and returned the traditional crown to the official Polish emblem, the white eagle. Communist and Solidarity members united to approve the changes by a vote of 374 to one, with 11 abstentions. The long struggle for liberation from the dead hand of Communism was over.

But there was little euphoria, for Solidarity had inherited a poisoned chalice. The immediate reward for the Polish people was economic disaster. For some time wages and prices had been chasing each other upwards in a dizzying spiral. Shortages had prompted the Government to increase prices, but workers almost immediately won higher wages, and these in turn led to fresh shortages. Rather than risk social unrest during the round table negotiations from February to April and during the parliamentary elections, the Government kept wages ahead of prices by printing more money, and by subsidising loss-making industries, particularly food and coal. Subsidies reached unprecedented levels: those on milk alone exceeded the defence budget. In July the Government had frozen wages and prices for one month, but it didn't work. Farmers anticipating a large increase in food prices in August reduced supplies. Then in August came the price deregulation by Rakowski's Government, an inevitable step which Solidarity implicitly accepted, even though for political reasons they gave the green light to protest strikes in Gdansk and elsewhere. The freeing of prices and the elimination of subsidies were designed to identify unprofitable enterprises and the next step was to close down the persistent loss-makers. Poland's external debt by now stood at $40 billion, more than half its gross national product, and monthly rates of inflation had been running at around 40 percent since August. Most of those who worked for the debased zloty earned the equivalent of less than $1000 a year.

In his inaugural address, Mazowiecki had hinted at the need for blood, sweat and tears. He admitted there would have to be unemployment, talked of setting up networks of employment offices and said there would be unemployment benefit, but only on a limited scale so as not to fuel inflation even more. In October the Solidarity-led Government launched an ambitious but highly unpopular economic plan to jump-start the economy. It reached a stabilisation agreement with the International Monetary Fund, which included the elimination of almost all remaining subsidies, a further devaluation of the zloty and wage controls to try to bring inflation under control. Economists expected real income to slump by 20 percent and hundreds of thousands of jobs to be lost. Parliament approved austerity reforms governing banking, taxation, currency joint ventures and the right of employers to make mass dismissals.

Shortly after Solidarity had accepted power, one of its elder statesmen had remarked on Polish TV that the movement might have gone into the Government too soon, and that taking the premiership might prove its 'gravest mistake ever'. But he added: 'We simply had no choice'. With responsibility for all the economic and financial ministries, Solidarity risked being blamed for all the economic problems that it had inherited and was at last attempting to solve. It found itself the object of the anger and frustration of workers who had been its natural constituency when it was in opposition.

Now a strange political transmutation began. On 13 October, Communist trade unionists marched through the streets of Warsaw to protest against the Solidarity Government's economic measures. In a bizarre reversal of roles, the OPZZ, a federation of unions set up as puppets by the Communist martial law regime after the suppression of Solidarity, warned of strong opposition among its seven million members to the drastic measures just announced. But there was no chance of the Communists using their bogus majority in the lower house to block the passage of the austerity measures, which had been agreed by the four Communist ministers in the Cabinet. Flushed out of power by Solidarity's overwhelming victory, the Communists were now desperately struggling to find a new niche to prevent themselves from being swept into oblivion.

The future of the PUWP had been the subject of intense internal argument since the elections. Several solutions were proposed, including dividing the Party into reformist and conservative groups. Rakowski, now First Secretary, argued in favour of this idea. But the Party rejected it, deciding instead to try to transform itself from a Stalinist-era party into a parliamentary party capable of functioning in a democracy. At a strained Central Committee meeting after Mazowiecki took power, one Politburo member, Leszek Miller, said they felt such a 'natural transformation' was essential. 'Otherwise we will inevitably be pushed to the margin of political life, and we will be dominated and removed not only by Solidarity, but also by other political forces', he said. Miller read out a report on a proposed future strategy for the Party prepared for the Central Committee by the Politburo. It was one of the frankest pieces of self-criticism ever drawn up in Eastern Europe, and amounted to a withering account of the Party's 45 years of rule. It confessed its responsibility for Stalinist crimes, ditched hoary old Communist slogans, such as the 'Dictatorship of the Proletariat' and declared that Communist rule in Eastern Europe had been 'erroneous' from the start.

It proposed that the Party disband itself and re-form under a new name with new policies. On economic policy, for instance, the document veered to the left of centre, arguing against wholesale privatisation of industry, but accepting that both forms of ownership should coexist. It proposed that the new Party should seek to expand links with the Socialist International while maintaining Poland's alliance to the Soviet Union, which, it said, guaranteed Poland's frontiers.

The document, with its denunciations of Communist doctrine, not unnaturally provoked conflict between reformers and hardliners, but a Congress of the 230-member PUWP Central Committee voted on 6 January to adopt the document and disband the Party. The PUWP thus became the second Communist Party in Eastern Europe to disband, following the example of the Party in Hungary. A new 'democratic socialist' Party stripped of Marxism was to be established, and the Central Committee authorised the 1637 Congress delegates to choose a name for the new party, offering six suggestions, such as Polish Social Democratic Party, Polish Labour or Polish Workers' Party.

Heir to Gomulka and Gierek: Aleksander Kwasniewski addresses the final congress of the Polish Communist Party in Warsaw before being elected Chairman. (Photo: Kok/Gamma)

Outside the Party Congress, anti-Communist demonstrators call for reform and democracy. (Photo: Kok/Gamma)

At a congress to set up a successor organisation the majority of delegates voted to found a new party to be called Social Democracy of the Polish Republic. It was to be committed to the concept of parliamentary democracy and the rule of law, and they elected an energetic liberal, Aleksander Kwasniewski, aged 36, as chairman. But around 100 Party reformers walked out, claiming that the new Party was simply the old one with a new label, and proceeded to set up a rival Party called the Social Democratic Union. The reformers were led by Tadeusz Fiszbach, deputy speaker of the Sejm, and a former Politburo member.

The Solidarity-led Government, meanwhile, had little time. Mazowiecki told West Germany's Labour and Social Affairs Minister, Norbert Bluem, during talks in Gdansk that it would have to prove itself within six months to a year or all that the country had achieved could collapse, 'After that time the public has got to see the first signs of improvement', he said. 'Otherwise things will start to fall apart.' Understandably, many Poles regard the future with trepidation. With empty shelves and sky high prices few were under any illusions that the transition to democracy would be other than painful.

HUNGARY
The long walk to Europe

4 November 1956	Soviet tanks crush Hungarian Uprising: reformist Government under Imre Nagy removed.
15 March 1986	3000 people demonstrate in Budapest on Hungary's unofficial independence day.
27 September 1987	Imre Pozsgay, Communist reformer, calls for a new constitution guaranteeing freedom of expression.
20–23 May 1988	At Party Conference, Kadar stands down as leader; Karoly Grosz succeeds.
26 January 1989	Government announces that Nagy and colleagues are to be reburied.
10 February 1989	Central Committee of Hungarian Communist Party accepts the need for a multi-party democracy.
May 1989	The barbed wire fence between Hungary and Austria, symbol of the Iron Curtain, is taken down.
16 June 1989	Nagy and colleagues reburied.
6 July 1989	Kadar dies; Supreme Court rules Nagy innocent.
11 September 1989	Hungary allows East Germans to leave across the border into Austria.
23 October 1989	New Hungarian Republic declared.
25 March 1990	Parliamentary elections.

'Twice this century, Hungary has tried to walk to Europe alone.' Endre Bojtar, a distinguished literary historian, was speaking in the spring of 1987 in Budapest. 'Both times we failed. Perhaps this time we will succeed, but carrying the Soviet Union on our back.' He was referring to 1918, when the Austro-Hungarian empire broke up at the end of World War I, and to the 1956 uprising, when Hungary briefly abolished the Communist Party's monopoly of power, and declared its intention of leaving the Warsaw Pact.

On 25 March 1990 the first round of a general election is due to be held, the first free elections in Hungary since November 1945. Though Hungarian democracy is still a fragile experiment, there is a good chance that a strong coalition government will emerge, with popular support as well as a majority of the votes.

15 March 1986: the crowd gathering around the statue to the poet Sandor Petofi, a hero of the 1848 revolution, buzzed with excitement as those present became aware of their own numbers – about 3000. Small numbers of students had kept alive the traditions of the country's unofficial independence day since it was dropped by the Communists after World War II, but this demonstration was exceptional, assisted by the warm spring sunshine, and a little help from the calendar – it was a Saturday.

Janos Kadar – ruler since he changed sides at the last moment in 1956, and was swept to power by Soviet tanks – was 73. Popular in the 1960s and 1970s for its relatively liberal character and the higher standard of living it had achieved, the regime Kadar led seemed ancient, but secure. The country was heavily in debt, and busy borrowing more to cushion the people from the inflation and unemployment which might otherwise reveal the weaknesses of the socialist economy. In 1985, at the XIIIth Congress of the Hungarian Socialist Workers Party, Kadar had pledged to maintain 'socialist achievements' like full employment and low inflation. The mass of the population saw Kadar as the latest in a line of 'good kings' and blamed his ministers for their grievances.

The crowd moved off slowly at noon, led by teenagers carrying a large tricolour Hungarian flag, horizontal bands of red, white and green. In the tall, narrow streets of the old town of Pest, their rhythmic clapping echoed. People came to their windows and balconies in amazement. For those old enough to remember 1956, there was anxiety. The marchers moved from one monument to the 1848 revolution to another, solemnly intoning patriotic hymns, and singing the Marseillaise. Speakers, barely audible without amplifying equipment, called for human rights for the Hungarian minority in Romania, and democracy at home. The police kept a low profile. By five in the afternoon, people were dispersing from Batthany Square on the Buda

side of the River Danube. A brief sit-down in the road, in protest at
the arrest of a girl gathering money to pay a samizdat publisher's fine,
was broken up swiftly by police moving in to write down identity card
numbers. In the evening, a smaller demonstration was ambushed by
police on the Chain bridge. Many were beaten with truncheons,
including bystanders, in what became known in the universities and
schools of the city as 'the battle of the bridge'.

'The only way to save socialism from the rubbish heap of history is
to allow other groups in society, eventually other parties, to compete
against the Party. Only if people choose it, of their own free will, is it
worth having', an official of KISZ, the Young Communist League,
who had been on the march later said.

Practical opposition to the regime in Hungary was either tiny, but
well organised – the 30 or so dissidents of the 'Democratic Opposition' – or large and completely unorganised – the 'establishment
opposition'. The Democratic Opposition published dense, devastating
analyses of the ills of society in their irregularly appearing journals.
They saw themselves, above all, as witnesses of a free press, and
human rights' violations, acting as normally as they could, until such a
time as free expression would be possible. Subjected to occasional
house searches, fines and confiscation of printing equipment, and
denied jobs, they were nevertheless part of the Kadarist establishment. The absence of political prisoners, apart from conscientious
objectors, was an important part of the Kadar Government's foreign
policy image, winning it grudging acceptance by Western governments.

The establishment opposition, a wide strata of teachers, journalists,
academics and other white collar professions, collaborated with the
Kadar regime but remained critical of it. They had two main political
grievances: the planned construction of a hydroelectric dam at
Nagymaros on the Danube, one of the most beautiful spots in a
country not well endowed with areas of great natural beauty, and the
situation of Hungarians in Transylvania. Together, they would become the two greatest catalysts of the Hungarian revolution, a
constant refrain over the coming months, drawing the 'middle classes'
back into political activism.

The economic grievances were less well defined. White collar
workers often earned less than blue collar workers, and they felt
financially and morally unrewarded for their work. Eighty percent of
the adult population had second or third jobs, supplementing their
meagre but guaranteed income in the state sector. People worked hard
to maintain the same standard of living for themselves and their
families. The collectivist rhetoric of the Party sat uneasily on an
individualistic people.

The poor were those who had to rely on their state job or pension alone for their income, the rich were the middlemen who could supply the fashionable Western goods which the state sector could not provide. The middle eight million of a population of 10.5 million earned roughly the same. The participants of the 15 March demonstration belonged to none of these groups. They were the rebellious young, many in their teens, whose strongest asset was that they were not afraid.

The official media published nothing about it. The smaller the circulation of a paper, or the more unsociable the hour of a broadcast, the closer to the opposition it tended to be. The weeklies, especially *HVG*, a magazine supposedly dedicated to the economy, excelled themselves in always pushing against the boundaries of the permissible. In the spring of 1986, two officially published journals, *Tisza Taj* the flagship of the Populists, and *Liget* were raided by police acting on the instructions of the agitation and propaganda department of the Party, and a whole edition pulped. Their crime had been to voice criticism of Janos Kadar personally.

There was one further, traditional division of the intelligentsia in Hungary, into the city-based, sometimes Jewish 'Urbanists', stressing values of individual liberty and justice, and the more rural 'Populists' who emphasised above all the 'survival of the Hungarian nation', from practical social questions like a falling birthrate, to the abstract 'Magyarsag' ('Hungarian-ness').

In June, Miss Hungary, 17-year-old Csilla Molnar, from a village near Lake Balaton, committed suicide. It was a national disaster. 'What kind of country is this', people asked one another, 'where our most beautiful daughter is driven to kill herself?' A film, 'Beautiful Girls', about the beauty contest, followed the story through to its tragic end, and was shown at cinemas all over the country. The suicide was a psychological blow for the Government. West European-style extravaganzas that summer, the country's first Formula One Grand Prix, and a concert by the British rock band 'Queen' in the People's Stadium, failed to erase the memory.

In July, a ban was announced on the works of a popular playwright, Istvan Csurka, because he had spoken out on the Transylvanian issue in a broadcast on 15 March on Radio Free Europe. Through the summer, the first waves of refugees arrived from Romania, largely belonging to the Hungarian minority. Many settled illegally in Hungary. Some were allowed quietly to leave across the Austrian border.

As October and the anniversary of the 1956 uprising approached, the authorities became more and more nervous. Secret policemen, one tall and thin in a leather raincoat, another short and fat in an anorak, the occupants of a green Lada with Ministry of the Interior number plates, were posted to guard the overgrown corner of a dreary suburban cemetery where the Prime Minister at the time of the uprising, Imre Nagy, and about 300 others also executed in the years after the Soviets put down the revolt were buried in unmarked graves. On the big day, 23 October, the thirtieth anniversary of the first demonstration that began the uprising, nothing happened. One 16-year-old girl placed a flag on the steps of the statue to Joseph Bem, another hero of 1848. She did this, she told secret policemen and Western journalists alike, for her father, who had taken part in the revolt, but mainly for herself. In the third district of the city, about 50 people gathered at the flat of a dissident publisher and burnt candles in memory of their revolution.

The Writers Union met for their five-yearly congress at the end of November, and demanded the reinstatement of the sacked editors of *Tisza Taj* and the lifting of Csurka's silence. Writer after writer complained about the state of the country. The Populists in particular, of whom Csurka was an acknowledged leader, were the most vocal on Transylvania, and on what was described as 'the retreat into illness', the high rate of alcoholism, suicide and heart disease which some claimed was the result of depriving the mass of the population of participation in political life. The writers were also spurred by their traditionally revolutionary role. In 1956 the uprising's demands were first formulated by a group of writers called the 'Petofi circle'.

In the elections to the union's steering committee all supporters of Janos Kadar lost their places. Kadar was furious and ordered the union destroyed. The Agitprop department of the Party was given the task of persuading those union members also in the Party to leave and set up a rival organisation. But a handful refused, placing their loyalty to the union first. 'Hunters have been sent to kill a mole', said an old lady whose past loyalty to the Party was unquestionable. 'But the water they poured down its hole has frozen and they are slipping over.' It was an embarrassing political defeat for Kadar.

In the summer of 1987, Karoly Grosz, an authoritarian but pragmatic Politburo member, was appointed Prime Minister with the task of tackling the economic crisis. What shocked him most on taking up the post was the extent of Party control over Government decisions, and the mess the economy was in. The money borrowed from the West had not been spent on modernising industry, which was having difficulty producing goods of high enough quality for Western markets, while the burden of servicing the debt had become ever more crippling. Grosz set about introducing a value added tax and a personal income tax, which had been proposed by economists for over a decade, and increasing the decision-making power of the Government at the expense of the Party. A less loyal servant of the Party could never have got away with it, but the orthodox Marxist-Leninists could only howl with dismay as they watched their influence being eroded by one of their own number.

Just before the September session of Parliament, which would decide on the new taxes, a broad cross-section of 100 intellectuals sent a letter to all 380 MPs. The essence of their message was that of the Boston tea party: 'no taxation without representation'. Only if serious political reform took place would the population be prepared to put up with the economic reforms, they argued. Political and economic reform programmes had been circulating for much of 1987. The most famous, *Turn-about and Reform*, had been published, in an abridged version, with a reply from Party economists. One of its authors, Laszlo Antal, had even been taken on to the Government team by Karoly Grosz, on the last stages of the tax plans. Antal's signature appeared in the 'Letter of 100'. Grosz's reaction to the letter was ambivalent. He mentioned it in public three times, once dismissing it roughly, another time taking it in his stride, and finally almost welcoming it.

Parliament accepted the new tax laws after a fierce debate – a personal triumph for Grosz. Three people were prevented by the Politburo from addressing Parliament: a representative of the Young Communists, a delegate from the official trade unions, and a radical Central Committee member, Imre Pozsgay.

Pozsgay was the most outspoken advocate of democracy in the Party, proof that its 'liberal' wing had not died after 1956, but had survived quietly under Kadar's cloak. Pozsgay had been appointed to the Central Committee in 1970, at a time when Kadar was still boldly introducing economic reforms, even though Hungarian troops had taken part in the suppression of the 1968 Prague Spring in Czechoslovakia. Other Warsaw Pact foreign ministers muttered darkly at that time within hearing distance of Hungarian officials: 'Budapest will be next'. The reforms in Hungary came to a stop. When they began again in the late 1970s, Pozsgay became Minister of Culture. In 1982 he was pushed sideways to be head of the Patriotic People's Front (PPF), which Imre Nagy had founded in 1954 in an attempt to give people outside the Party a voice in the nation's affairs. The PPF had never been given a chance to fulfil that role. Kadar's own tolerance was a personal one, issued at a whim and just as easily withdrawn. He left the system of institutions, created in the 1950s, much as he found them. Pozsgay set about turning the PPF into an umbrella under which reformers, inside and outside the Party, could gather to discuss ideas of increasing democracy. There was no such space in the Party itself.

Hardliners like Janos Berecz were constantly plotting Pozsgay's downfall. He was rarely allowed to publish in the national press, which Berecz controlled, and then never on political reform. But Kadar protected him from their wrath. A keen chess player, Kadar's skill in politics had been to play off people below him, one against another, and so ensure that his own power remained secure. Pozsgay had become Kadar's 'democratic card', to use against Berecz and the others if they seemed to be getting too big for their boots. Prevented from speaking to the country through Parliament, and encouraged by the changes taking place in the Soviet Union under Gorbachov, Pozsgay launched his own campaign for democracy outside the Party.

On 27 September 1987, a meeting of mainly Populist intellectuals was held in 'a wedding-tent atmosphere' at a farm near the village of Lakitelek in central Hungary. Imre Pozsgay was the guest of honour, and used the occasion to call for a new constitution guaranteeing freedom of expression. Other speakers called for a reform programme to be drawn up to deal with the crisis 'in every sphere of life', from education to the economy.

At the end of the day, the Hungarian Democratic Forum was founded, a talk-shop rather than an organisation, which would have been illegal. A poem was read out, which could have been the Populists' manifesto: 'Don't be sad my friend, those who push aside from the road will go nowhere. For we are the wheels of the cart. Without us, there is no Hungarian-ness and no Revolution.'

One feature marred the excitement of the day. Few from the Urbanist circles of the intelligentsia had been invited, and none of the leading dissidents. Several of those who had, stayed away in protest. The two groups had met earlier, at the village of Monor near Budapest in 1985, and it had appeared for a moment that their old arguments might be buried for the sake of political change. But Lakitelek was conceived by its organisers – among them Istvan Csurka – as a follow-on not to Monor, but to the Writers' Union victory over the Party. Some argued privately that the leading Urbanist dissidents, publishers of samizdat like Janos Kis and Miklos Haraszti, could not appear at the same gathering as Pozsgay, as Pozsgay would then be kicked out of the Party for certain, and the embryonic democratic forces in the country would have lost their man closest to the throne. Whatever the motives, the bitter division between Populists and Urbanists was reinforced.

Karoly Grosz went to Bonn and came back with a loan of one billion DM and a BMW for his personal use. His hold over the Government was unchallenged, but his brief popularity in the country was over. Small things indicated which way the wind was blowing. One evening in a beer-hall in Buda, when Grosz was appearing on television, a man strode forward with a bread-knife which he jabbed playfully at the screen. Everybody laughed. 'What we need in this country is a little Gorbachov', an old man muttered. Grosz wasn't such a man, but Pozsgay might be.

A witch-hunt began against Pozsgay within the Party, the aim of which was to persuade Kadar to have him sent off as ambassador to somewhere – anywhere – in Africa. Pozsgay counter-attacked, touring the country speaking to workers, managers, students, priests, and anyone else who would listen to him – all largely unreported by the media. At the Technical University in Budapest, a student asked him: 'Are you the Imre Nagy of the 1980s?' 'I always wonder when people ask me that, what their own opinion is of Imre Nagy', he replied to applause. A loose and unlikely alliance developed between Grosz and Pozsgay. Grosz had alienated his old supporters in the Party, but held power. Pozsgay had support in the country, but little power. They were useful to each other.

In January 1988, 600 people gingerly approached the Jurta Theatre in People's Park in Budapest for the first meeting of the Hungarian Democratic Forum (HDF) in the capital. No policemen emerged from the bushes, though one in plain clothes, present at every unofficial gathering, was always the first to vote for the radical motions proposed. The subject for discussion this time was parliamentary democracy. There were Party members among the speakers, and in the audience. Every speech was applauded equally enthusiastically, almost regardless of content; the audience were in fact applauding themselves, simply for being there.

Karoly Grosz and others from Janos Kadar's own circle, alarmed by the state of the economy, persuaded Kadar to agree to a special Party conference in May 1988. The last 'conference', as opposed to 'congress', had been held in 1957 to confirm Kadar in his post as Party leader. The aim of this one would be to oust him, because of his opposition to market-oriented reforms. A battle raged within the Party through the spring of 1988 over what powers the conference should have. A blurred three-way split was visible within the Party, with Kadar's supporters leading the hardliners, Grosz the centrists and Pozsgay the reformers. The groups were defined as much by their judgement of the past as by their policies for the future. Now that 'the power', as it was known, acknowledged the seriousness of the economic crisis, it was logical to ask 'When did we go wrong?' and 'Who is responsible?' The hardliners were prepared to look as far back as 1983, the centrists to 1972, and the reformers to 1956 or even 1948 – the year Communists seized power.

For all the frenetic activity in the plethora of new political groups outside the Party, the demonstration of the unofficial independence day on 15 March 1988 drew less than 10,000 people. The HDF met again in March to discuss Transylvania. The refugees pouring across the border for the past 18 months now totalled somewhere between 15 and 30 thousand, most of whom were in Hungary illegally, staying with friends, relatives, or church groups, afraid from one day to the next that a slight change in Government policy would have them rounded up and sent back. Many had risked their lives to cross the border and an unknown number had died in the attempt. The authorities slowly and reluctantly began to acknowledge the existence of the refugees, and to provide money and services to help.

The New March Front was formed, of 20 leading figures from across the political spectrum. Their composition was more significant than their programme. They included Miklos Vasarhelyi, former press secretary to Imre Nagy, and a father figure of the democratic opposition, and Rezso Nyers, Central Committee member of the HSWP. Their existence alone was a political ultimatum to Janos Kadar: Get out or reform. A full-scale rebellion against Kadar now gathered steam at local level within the Party. The 'historic opportunity' of a benevolent despot in Moscow needed to be taken advantage of, reform Communists realised, while most outside the Party still doubted the honesty of Gorbachov's intentions. Kadar launched his final manifesto, a 'blueprint' for the Party Conference in May, spelling out how far he was prepared to go in democratisation. It was not very far. One Party cell after another demolished it, and the Party newspaper *Nepszabadsag* had to publish their criticisms. The Academy of Sciences rejected it, closely followed by Imre Pozsgay's PPF. The Party cell at the Karl Marx University of Economics in Budapest published the first fateful call for the resignation of both Government and Party leadership.

At the end of March, a group of law students founded FIDESZ, the Federation of Democratic Youth, from the outset the most militant wing of the 'democratic forces'. On 6 April the hardliners finally persuaded Kadar to act. Four radical reformers close to Pozsgay were expelled from the Party because of their attendance at meetings of the HDF. FIDESZ was declared illegal. It was a shot across Pozsgay's bows, but it was far too late. A snowball was gathering momentum in the political circles of the country, though the vast majority of the population was completely unaware of it. The snowball was rolling straight at Janos Kadar.

In early May the first independent trade union, the white-collar Democratic Union of Scientific Workers, was founded and the democratic opposition set up an above-ground political organisation of their own, the Network of Free Initiatives (NFI). They exchanged observers with the HDF, but both turned down the invitation to join the other. The Populist/Urbanist split was being institutionalised, even before a democratic state could emerge.

The Party Conference was due to begin on 20 May, a Friday. Two days earlier Miklos Vasarhelyi told *The Observer* that a senior official in the Foreign Ministry, Gyula Horn, had that morning taken Kadar a personal message from Mikhail Gorbachov. The gist of the message was 'Thank you for your services, please step down now, in the interests of your country'. Until that moment, Kadar had stubbornly resisted all efforts from within his own Party to remove him. The Russians had put him in. It was left to the poor Russians to get him out.

The Party Conference was a tense, three-day affair in the Ferenc Rozsa assembly hall of the Construction Workers' Union, just off Heroes Square. Kadar made two long, rambling, almost nonsensical speeches, on the Friday and Sunday mornings, neither of them mentioning his intention to step down. Secret ballots were held late on Sunday morning. One-third of the 100-member Central Committee were replaced. Most of the Politburo were removed. Karoly Grosz was elected as new General Secretary of the Party. Pozsgay and Nyers became members of the Politburo. Kadar received the new, honorary post of 'Party President'. 'We have already gone further than in Prague in 1968', Pozsgay told a press conference. 'We are setting out now across uncharted waters', said Nyers.

The first and most striking change for most Hungarians was in the media. Journalists had been in the forefront of the new movements pressing for change. The police, a willing servant of the old guard, were rather slower to react to the new situation. On 16 June, a few hundred people gathered in the centre of Budapest to mark the anniversary of Imre Nagy's execution, and several leading figures in the Network of Free Initiatives were beaten up and arrested. Larger demonstrations against the Nagymaros dam, and against the regime of Nicolai Ceausescu in Romania, passed off peacefully.

Grosz met Ceausescu in the Romanian border town of Arad, and failed to win any concessions, to the anger of ordinary Hungarians. The Foreign Ministry in Budapest mentioned for the first time the possibility of a partial Soviet withdrawal.

With Kadar gone, the events of 1956 came back to haunt his successors. The 'legitimacy' of Kadar's 32 years in office depended on the belief that if he had not complied with the Soviet Union's wishes, a more Stalinist leader would have been chosen, and the past three decades would have been a much harsher period for the Hungarian people. But the moment Kadar donned his dark green overcoat and brown trilby, and strolled away from the conference centre, that legitimacy evaporated. Curiously, however, nobody else in Hungary could claim any better credentials. No one had actually been chosen by the people. The Democratic Opposition, in whatever guise, were basically a bunch of friends, some of them former Marxists and

Maoists, with widely disparate political beliefs, united by a common commitment to a free press, and by their own bravery and good reputation for standing up for democracy when the vast majority of the population were content to work hard for their own personal gain. But they had no more been chosen by the people as the opposition, than the Communists had been chosen to rule the nation.

The HSWP in power was never completely discredited in the eyes of the population, as the Polish Communist Party had been. At the peak of his popularity, Kadar might even have won a free election. Even now, they might win 30 percent of a free vote against the other new and inexperienced political groups. Pozsgay and Nyers set about trying to transform the HSWP into a liberal and democratic party for which people would actually vote, if in due course other parties were formed and free elections held. The HDF, NFI, FIDESZ and others spent the autumn of 1988 trying to keep up the pressure on the HSWP, and working out their own political organisation and programmes. Without the remarkably free access which they were now given to the official media, that would barely have been possible. Two new papers were also founded, *Hitel* for the HDF and *Reform*, a glossy, mass circulation weekly, with a mixture of pornography, scandal and pro-democracy articles. Pozsgay for his part warned that the moment for the spontaneous forming of new parties had not yet been reached and that conservative forces within the HSWP were still strong enough to organise a backlash, if provoked. In private talks, he told the leaders of FIDESZ that two subjects still remained taboo – the rehabilitation of Imre Nagy and the withdrawal of Hungary from the Warsaw Pact.

'For the first time, the opposition could get more support than the Party', a senior newspaper editor said. 'No one can guarantee control any longer without the use of administrative [meaning police] measures.' Grosz was leaning towards the conservatives in his own party. He admired Margaret Thatcher, he had said earlier, 'for the consistent way in which she pursued policies which she believed were in the best interests of her country'. At the end of November, in a speech to 10,000 HSWP activists, Grosz spoke of 'counter-revolutionary forces', and warned of the danger of 'chaos, anarchy and white terror'. The whole time, however, the carpet was being pulled from under his feet.

Parliament approved a new Company Law, with enormous ideological implications. Private share ownership was approved for the first time, the limit on the number of employees at a private firm raised from 30 to 500, and foreign firms were permitted to buy entire Hungarian companies. It must have seemed hard to reinstate single party orthodoxy in society, when the whole economic basis of that ideology was being thrown out of another window.

There were light moments too. At the Seoul Olympics, Hungary won 11 gold medals, placing the country sixth in the world. A bumper wheat crop, sold to the United States for hard currency, eased the economic crisis for a few months. Budapest was once as famous for its horse chestnuts as Paris for its plane trees. That autumn, there seemed almost as many shiny conkers in the street as young demonstrators.

Foreign policy, the art of maintaining maximum links with the West without upsetting Moscow, had been one of the successes of the Kadar years. On a visit to West Germany, Gyula Horn became the first Warsaw Pact representative to address the North Atlantic Assembly of Nato. The Soviet Union should withdraw its forces from Hungary, he told them bluntly. He welcomed the possibility of a multi-party system, but for the time being, unity was more important, he said.

To the disgust of the population, Parliament approved the dam with a large majority, Pozsgay voting in favour, and Nyers abstaining. Karoly Grosz gave up his post of Prime Minister, to concentrate on leading the Party. An ambitious, reform-minded technocrat, Miklos Nemeth, became Prime Minister.

Kalman Kulcsar, the new Justice Minister, raised eyebrows with a statement that the way was now clear for multi-party democracy in Hungary, though the Party were still bitterly divided on the issue. This would come about in two stages. First a Law on Association, to go before Parliament before Christmas, then a Law on Parties, expected in 1989. To help this process along, Kulcsar sent officials from his ministry to contact relatives of those executed in 1956, to ask if they would like them to receive decent burial 'for humanitarian reasons'. No single question was so loaded with political implications for the future of Hungary.

The Network of Free Initiatives, in order to hold Kulcsar to his words, reformed themselves as a political party, the Association of Free Democrats (AFD). The Smallholders' Party and the Social Democrats also reformed. A demonstration on 15 November, the anniversary of the Brasov protests against President Ceausescu in Romania in 1987, was violently broken up by police in Budapest. Gorbachov addressed the United Nations, promising unilateral troop cuts by the Warsaw Pact. In mid-December, Parliament met, eager to rescue its soiled reputation as a serious institution by throwing out all three variants of the budget proposed by the Government, and opting instead for a fourth variant, cutting defence spending by 17 percent and slashing millions from the state support given to the HSWP. In an attempt to appease his own critics, Karoly Grosz told Parliament that as from 1989, 15 March would become a national holiday. In the excitement, the new Law of Associations was postponed until January.

1989 began as it promised to continue for the Hungarian population, with economic austerity and political drama. Big price rises left the poor digging deeper in their purses for the smallest denomination aluminium coins, and the poorest searching the waste bins of the capital for bottles on which to reclaim a small deposit. FIDESZ launched a successful campaign at a local level to unseat those MPs who had spoken in favour of the Nagymaros dam, by gathering signatures against them. The Law on Associations was duly passed by Parliament, legitimising groups who had long been active anyway. Karoly Grosz conceded that his preference for a one party system had been defeated. The fact that the new Party Law would not be ready until August left open a 'window of suspicion' to independent groups, that some trick might yet be employed by the HSWP to hang on to power. On 26 January, the Government announced that Imre Nagy and his colleagues would be re-buried, but stopped short of saying they had been falsely tried. The same day, the Soviet Union told Hungary that the promised troop withdrawals would begin in June.

Two days later, Imre Pozsgay gave the preliminary findings of the historical subcommittee on which he had been sitting to re-evaluate the events of the last 40 years. 1956 could not be regarded as a 'counter-revolution' he said. It had been, in fact, 'a popular uprising'. Party conservatives were outraged. Karoly Grosz called an emergency meeting of the Central Committee of the HSWP for 10 February. The Writers' Union and the independent groups expressed their support for Pozsgay, with the Free Democrats going further, saying 1956 had been a 'popular revolution'.

For a few days, the whole political future of the country hung in the balance. The meeting would prove to be the last chance for the conservatives to claw back from the brink of a Western-style democracy. If Pozsgay's statement, and the subcommittee report, were accepted by the Party, they would have little choice but to open the floodgates. The political rehabilitation of Imre Nagy would surely follow. Their Party's rule for the last 32 years would be declared illegitimate. They would have little choice but to give up their 'leading role'. Could the Party even continue to exist?

Grosz would say later that he wished he had taken the opportunity then to throw Pozsgay out of the Party leadership. But Pozsgay survived. His position was accepted, and a compromise struck. The Party issued a statement accepting his interpretation of 1956, and agreeing that a multi-party system would now be necessary in Hungary. Coming from Government representatives like Kulcsar, the idea had seemed a good one, but improbable in the view of most Hungarians. They knew that real power still lay with the Party. But now the Party itself was saying the same. For the first time, disappointed so often in the past, ordinary Hungarians sensed that history might for once be on their side. The same day, a senior Soviet academician Oleg Bogmolov told a Moscow news conference that a neutral, democratic Hungary would be acceptable to the Soviet Union.

'Our aim is not to hand over power, but to share it', an HSWP official said, as the Party published its draft policy on the gradual transition to a multi-party system. A week earlier, round table talks had started in Poland between the Solidarity movement and the Communist Party. Some kind of 'permanent forum of consultations' was envisaged in Hungary too.

Stark contradictions remained, both in the written statements of the Party, and in the public pronouncements of its leaders. Opposition groups expressed outrage whenever they saw the word 'socialism' used. According to one statement, the Party wanted to play a 'determining role' for the transition period, leading to elections in 1990. And Grosz seemed at one moment to take everything back, by saying that cooperation with other political groups was only possible if they accepted socialism. The truth was that the Party had not yet surrendered, but it had relaxed its brittle grip on power, thanks to popular pressure, the bravery of men like Pozsgay, the need for Western investment to rescue the country from bankruptcy, and the green light from the Soviet Union.

The progress that had been made in 12 months was clear when 80,000 people from 31 independent groups joined the 15 March demonstration. It was so good natured and orderly that newly laid flower beds escaped unscathed. The HSWP leadership had expressed the hope that the Party and opposition could celebrate the day together, but this was turned down flat by the opposition. The bruises of past demonstrations were still too sore. Only Pozsgay, in the west Hungarian town of Gyor, had the honour of being allowed to address a joint rally of Party and opposition. In Budapest, the HSWP celebrated alone, in the early hours of the morning, so as to be out of the way by the time the mass of the demonstrators arrived.

Few cities are more convenient for a patriotic pilgrimage. The crowd that gathered that spring morning started at the monument to Petofi, the hero-poet of the failed fight for Hungarian independence in 1848 who was killed by a Russian bullet. They followed along the Danube towards Freedom Square, and then to the monument to Kossuth, the leader in 1848, whose bronze right hand admonishes the neo-Gothic Parliament. In Hungary, they seemed to be saying, the surest way forward is to remember the past.

Opposition speakers were confident. History has pronounced its sentence on the system called Socialism, the crowd at Kossuth's feet were told by Janos Kis, a sociologist who had done much to provide the opposition with intellectual fuel. That Kis could say such things without fear of police intervention was evidence of the regime's surrender of control over public debate.

Before setting down to negotiate with the HSWP, the opposition groups met to work out a common position on a timetable to lead to free elections in 1990. Their visions of a future Hungary clearly diverged. The HDF believed in a 'third way', between capitalism and Communism, a specifically Hungarian model of democracy. The Free Democrats whole-heartedly embraced Western parliamentary democracy and the free market, but were divided themselves between a liberal, and a social democratic faction. The Forum believed some kind of coalition agreement could be worked out with the HSWP before the election, and the Free Democrats argued that this could only be contemplated after an election, when the different parties had had a chance to test their strengths in front of the electorate. All parties agreed that the abandonment of the Nagymaros dam was a precondition for serious negotiations with the HSWP.

Miklos Nemeth's Government was making serious mistakes in its economic policy, and looking even more foolish by admitting them. Measures to stop the drain of privately held hard currency to the electronics shops of Austria were announced, but left one more bank holiday weekend free before they came into effect. Half a million Hungarians were estimated to have poured over to Austria that weekend, one in 20 of the population. Various opposition proposals that the Government and Parliament be dissolved, and a caretaker Government formed with opposition participation, came to nothing. Janos Berecz lost his place in the Politburo, Gyula Horn became Foreign Minister, and 'reform circles' sprang up within the HSWP to speed up the pace of change. Just as Grosz had forced a Party Conference the previous year, so the reform circles, backing Pozsgay, demanded that the five-yearly Party Congress scheduled for 1990 be brought forward to the autumn of 1989. Their aim was to draw up a credible policy for the Party, corresponding to the changes in the country, and to remove Grosz as leader, seeing him as the main obstacle to their plans. Pozsgay was by now warning of a power vacuum, left by the Party giving up power before the opposition were ready to assume it. He suggested that the post of President be created, and somebody found to fill it, to act as a landmark, a piece of solid ground in such a rapidly changing political landscape.

The growing confidence of the opposition groups, especially of the Free Democrats, had caused a hardening of their stance. Pozsgay had always been quite close to the Democratic Forum, thanks to his own country background. The Free Democrats began to speak darkly of a secret pact between the Forum and Pozsgay, to carve up power between the HDF and the HSWP and to get its own candidate, Pozsgay, elected and so hang on to some of their power. There is little evidence for this. Pozsgay was seeing himself less and less as a Party man, while the paranoia of the years underground was colouring the world-view of the Free Democrats.

But Pozsgay, too, was starting to make mistakes. The lynch pin of reform for so long, he found it hard to imagine the process continuing without him playing a pivotal role. He also made a serious error in underestimating the growing support in the country for the Free Democrats.

Only Hungarian foreign policy ran smoothly. In May the barbed wire fence along the Austrian border – the very symbol of the Iron Curtain – was taken down. The implications for the other countries of the Warsaw Pact were breathtaking. Not since the Berlin Wall went up in the early 1960s had it been possible for East Europeans to stroll westward at sunset, without fear of arrest. The governments of East Germany and Czecholsovakia would now face a choice – either to prevent their tourists visiting Hungary in their hundreds of thousands, or to risk losing them.

As the date for the reburial of Imre Nagy, 16 June, approached there seemed no limit to Hungarian independence. The Soviet Union began withdrawing its troops, and Hungarian television screened a two-part interview with Alexander Dubcek. The Czech Government protested, and the Hungarians told them to mind their own business. In May, Miklos Nemeth took the remarkable, but enormously popular decision to suspend work on the Nagymaros dam. Rezso Nyers had been trying to persuade him to do this for months. The Czech Government, and the Austrians too, who between them had put up much of the money, were furious. Hungary was alienating her neighbours to such an extent that the more cautious political analysts in Budapest began warning of the danger of a resurgence of the 'little entente' of Czechoslovakia, Romania and Austria after World War I.

Janos Kadar, of whom little had been heard for many months, resigned from the Party presidency in May, ostensibly on grounds of ill health. Soon afterwards, the HSWP announced that Imre Nagy had indeed been unlawfully executed. For Pozsgay, it was a vindication. For the population, it was yet another example of a clumsy, resented Party being five steps behind everybody else.

A quarter of a million people filed solemnly through Heroes Square on 16 June, in front of six coffins containing the exhumed remains of Imre Nagy, his Defence Minister Pal Maleter, and three of their colleagues in the revolution. The Hungarian people honoured men who had put their country before their Party allegiances. The sixth coffin was empty, a symbolic gesture for the Historical Justice Committee who organised the events of the day, to represent all the others who died in the course of the revolution. The coffins lay on the steps of the main Exhibition Hall. On one side of the square was the

Yugoslav Embassy where Nagy initially took refuge after the Soviet invasion. Assured a safe passage, Nagy and his colleagues were arrested almost immediately they left the embassy grounds. Watching the ceremony on behalf of the Government were Imre Pozsgay and Miklos Nemeth. There were no official representatives of the HSWP, but there were diplomats from all but the most hardline Communist states. Many in the crowd wondered what Janos Kadar was doing on that day. Black flags flew in the streets, and at noon church bells rang out all over the country. Viktor Orban, the fiery rhetorician of FIDESZ, hoped that this day would have the same effect in Hungary as the Pope's visit had had on Poland in 1980. The men were reburied in the same distant corner of a distant cemetery in which they had been found – unrecognisably re-landscaped.

Round table talks began in typically ingenious Hungarian manner, on a triangular basis, with the opposition round table on one side, the Party on another, and official state organisations like the trade unions on another. 'We don't want to share power. We want the people to decide who runs the country', said Imre Konya, spokesman of the opposition. At the second round of talks on 21 June, Imre Pozsgay promised 'fully free and democratic elections' at which the HSWP would compete on equal terms with the other parties.

At a meeting of the Central Committee of the HSWP, Rezso Nyers began to advise caution, alarmed by the prospect of the Party splitting up into different factions. In an attempt to heal the divisions, a new four-man presidium was formed, of Groz, Pozsgay, Nemeth and Nyers, with Nyers in nominal control, to steer the Party up to the Congress in October. For 18 months now, Myers had worked away behind the scenes, persuading the Party to accept the loss of its power. Though Pozsgay's role had been more public, Nyers was the great architect of the 1988–89 reforms. At the end of June, the Democratic Forum, after a long and bitter internal argument, finally declared that it too was now a political party.

On 6 July Janos Kadar died, aged 77. He had been seriously ill in hospital for several days. A few hours later, the Supreme Court which had been instructed to review the Nagy trial declared him and those tried with him completely innocent. The man, and the system he helped to create, died on the very same day.

Then the US President, George Bush, arrived. Thunder and lightning rolled over Kossuth Square as Bush spoke. Clearly astonished by the pace of change, he spent much of his visit congratulating people. Viktor Orban told him nothing had changed. Pozsgay told him everything had.

Tens of thousands attended the second state funeral in a week. For many years of his life, Kadar was liked by ordinary Hungarians. 'We have a lot to thank him for', was a commonly held view. Most agreed also that he had held on to power too long, partly because of the mess he had left the country in, but also for his own sake, to spare him the humiliation of seeing his paper castle collapse. From the second half of July, the half-expected flood of refugees began, but all from East Germany rather than Czechoslovakia. Many just ran across the border. One was tragically shot in what appeared to be an accident. Many more, afraid to risk crossing the border illegally, even without the barbed wire, overflowed campsites which turned into refugee camps. The numbers involved – less than 10,000 – were smaller than those of the refugees from Romania, but the effect of the exodus on the East German regime of Erich Honecker was dramatic. After weeks of hectic diplomacy, Gyula Horn resolved the East German refugee crisis in the simplest way possible, by allowing them to leave for the West. The West German Government issued passports to more than 6000 waiting in Hungarian refugee camps. A week later Miklos Nemeth said the border would now stay open permanently.

The round table talks broke down briefly, with each side accusing the others of inflexibility. The opposition were united on the need for the HSWP cells in the workplace to be disbanded, and political activity there banned. The logic of this argument was clear. The last thing the economy needed now was for the factories, the main centres of HSWP power, to become the front line of the political struggles. At the beginning of September, Pozsgay gave in to the opposition's demands. Once again the HSWP was scandalised, and a crisis meeting was held. This was their last bastion. This time, Pozsgay and the radicals simply could not take the Party with them, and they were defeated; the prospect of a split into two or three different parties loomed larger.

A second divisive issue was the question of the presidency. The round table finally agreed that a presidential election would be held in November, with parliamentary elections three months later, using a complicated mixture of proportional representation and constituencies similar to that used in West Germany. The Free Democrats and FIDESZ refused to sign the agreement, but decided not to use their veto either. A President, directly elected, was a recipe for a return to totalitarian rule, they said, and they would have nothing to do with it.

At the end of the month, Parliament passed legislation paving the way for the establishment at last of a 'state of law', in which people's rights were protected by the law and all institutions answerable to it. This had been the vision guiding all people of democratic conviction in the country for the past two or three years. The six bills introduced covered the establishment of political parties, electoral law, the setting up of a Constitutional Court, and reform of the penal code.

Early in October, the HSWP met for their fourteenth and final

Congress. Like sleigh-borne travellers chased by wolves, the 1276 delegates gathered at the Novotel conference centre to argue about what more could be sacrificed to appease the ravenous pursuers. In the past 16 months the Communists had chucked out an astonishing list of treasured possessions. First they abandoned their once-venerated leader, Janos Kadar, and shed scarcely a tear. Since then, almost nothing had been deemed too precious to abandon. The leading role of the Party? Let the beasts have it. The centrally controlled economy? They had been almost pleased to toss it out.

Pozsgay was under considerable pressure from his own supporters to make a clean break with the Party and lead a new one, once it became clear that they were not strong enough to win over the HSWP. The equation had been further complicated by the emergence of Miklos Nemeth as an even more radical reformer than Pozsgay, despite his previous high rank under Kadar. While Pozsgay and Nyers were split over tactics, a personal animosity between Pozsgay and Nemeth made it almost impossible for them to talk to one another. Nemeth, by 'out-reforming Pozsgay' may have been trying to secure his own political career in a future coalition government. In the end, the plans of each failed.

The radicals decisively lost the first vote, on abolishing Party branches in the workplace, with Pozsgay, Nemeth, and Horn voting on the losing side. The reason for their defeat was Rezso Nyers. 'I go with the Party towards success, or failure', he had said in January 1988. He was determined that a split be avoided, and that the Party should stay together under a new name, the Hungarian Socialist Party (HSP). The 'Workers' in 'HSWP' were quietly dropped.

At this critical point, Pozsgay decided against leading a breakaway faction. The new Party had, after all, adopted his programme, though he had been contradicted on the issue of Party cells in the workplace. The expected walkout of hardliners did not take place. For the time being, they were happy to sit out of the rain in the shelter of the old Party building. One factor influencing Pozsgay may have been his hopes of landing a state, rather than a Party post – that of President, where he could play the role of an arbitrator, or elder statesman above mere party squabbles. Rezso Nyers became leader of the new Socialist Party, with a large majority.

The Hungarian people, who had looked forward with some expectation to the Congress, hoping to see clear parties emerge from it, were disappointed. 'Pozsgay sided with the Party, instead of with the people', an independent trade unionist said. The new Party still occupied the old Party building, the 'White House' beside the Danube with the statues of Marx and Engels by the flower stalls outside, and the mural of hard-working proletarians in the entrance hall. Karoly Grosz might have fallen from the leadership, but Rezso Nyers seemed to have inherited his caution. 'This is not just a collapse, this is a melt-down', said a Party official who three years earlier had welcomed the idea of a multi-party system. What surprised him most were the personal animosities between the different leaders.

A week later, Parliament voted to ban the functioning of parties in the workplace, leaving the new Socialist Party looking extremely foolish for taking such a firm stand on an issue which was no longer in its power. At the same session of Parliament, a new 'Hungarian Republic' was proclaimed by Miklos Nemeth, who announced that the 'Republic Day' would be 23 October, the following week. For the third time in six months the rulers offered a specific day for national reconciliation. Parliament ordered the abolition of the Workers' Militia, a 60,000 strong band of veteran Party members with access to weapons, and the passing over of HSWP property to the nation.

A day for celebration: in Kossuth Square in Budapest, thousands turned out to celebrate the proclamation of the new Hungarian Republic on 23 October 1989. (Photo: Tamas Revesz/GLMR)

In the east of Hungary, a local branch of the Free Democrats began to unravel the compromise over the presidency. It proposed to the national leadership of the Party in Budapest that signatures be gathered to force a referendum against the presidential election planned for 25 November. The leadership hesitated, then accepted the idea. 100,000 signatures would be needed. Four questions appeared on the petition: people were asked if they would like to vote on the timing of the presidential election, the eviction of the HSWP from the workplace, the redistribution of HSWP property, and the abolition of the Workers' Militia. The petition was enthusiastically circulated around the country by young Party activists, especially those in FIDESZ, and gathered, hardly surprisingly, twice the necessary number of signatures, even before the parliamentary session could itself decide on the last three points. A referendum now legally had to be held.

The proclamation of the new Hungarian Republic, on 23 October, was a day for the opposition to savour. All day people listened to speeches across the city, in the squares, outside the radio building. At 7 pm Kossuth Square in front of Parliament was still crowded with people, many sitting quietly alone, in front of candles burning low, or talking in small clusters. On a street corner almost opposite Party headquarters a stall sold books on the events of 1956 and a single by a band called 'East' entitled 'Wind of Change'. The atmosphere in the streets, the couples, the lonely people reluctant to go home, resembled the aftermath of a rock festival.

The referendum campaign, Hungary's first free vote for 44 years, was almost a shambles. The Democratic Forum, stung by charges that it really supported Pozsgay, not its own presidential candidate, Lajos Für, urged a complete boycott in the hope that the necessary 50 percent turnout would not be reached. The Free Democrats, campaigning brilliantly, urged the voters to say yes to each of the four propositions, while the Socialists urged one no (to the postponement of the presidential election) and three yesses. On a chilly autumnal day, 51 percent turned out to vote. Snow fell heavily in Budapest within minutes of the poll booths closing that Sunday evening. The result was a hair's breadth victory for the four yesses. There would be no presidential election before the parliamentary election. The Free Democrats had arrived as a serious force in Hungarian politics. Pozsgay accepted defeat graciously. 'Perhaps now the Free Democrats will lose their obsession that we are trying to hang on to power', he told a press conference.

Miklos Nemeth's Government struggled on through the winter with the speaker of Parliament, Matyas Szuro, as nominal head of state. Parliamentary elections were set for 25 March. The Socialists, a leadership without a membership, did badly in the opinion polls. The Free Democrats went from strength to strength, and the Democratic Forum consolidated the support they had built up over the last two years.

As the elections approached, the two parties, aware that they might afterwards have to form a coalition, softened their attacks on one another. The Smallholders' Party registered a continued loyalty vote with the rural population.

The creation of the Hungarian Republic provided a chance for national reconciliation. (Photo: Christian Vioujard/Gamma)

Hungary went into the general election of 1990 with over 50 parties, but with many of the population far from convinced that any of them represented their interests. Complex coalition-building appeared to be the likeliest outcome.

All parties were agreed on the need for harsh austerity measures which may leave up to half a million people unemployed. Industry cannot be modernised and made competitive overnight, and meanwhile one million jobs depend on unprofitable trade with other former Eastern bloc neighbours. Initial alarm about West German money going to help East Germany instead of Hungary might be soothed in the long term by more investment in Hungary by other West European countries, eager to offset the weight of a new Germany.

About a million people already live at or below what sociologists have defined as the minimum subsistence level. Hungary will not be able to afford a welfare state. What may emerge, however is a mixture of state, private and church institutions which will manage to create a welfare net of sorts. The divisions between the rich and poor are bound to grow wider, and with that comes the risk of serious social conflict. The old trade union structure has largely collapsed, without a new one having risen in its place, so any workers' protests which do take place are likely to be angry and disorganised. Equally, if the Government which emerges from the elections proves strong and united enough to formulate clear economic and social programmes, the mass of the population may support it in the hope of better times in the future.

The smallest rewards may in the end go to those partly responsible for bringing the change about, the reformist wing of the old HSWP. But having survived the onslaught of the Stalinists so long, it would be surprising if they cannot survive a spell in a rather different political wilderness. Or perhaps a 'grand coalition' – the elusive 'national reconciliation', much hoped for but never achieved before the elections – will come about after them.

In late 1989, research by the sociologist Rudolf Andorka suggested that the alcoholism and suicide rate in the country had fallen dramatically. The 'silent majority' might still be silent, but it appeared they were at least a little happier.

Hungary had shifted in the last years of the 1980s from being a 'greenhouse of reform' to being a perpetrator and encourager of popular revolution – in East Germany, Czechoslovakia, Romania and the Soviet Union. 'Our tragedy in the past was that the nations of this region tried to liberate themselves one by one', said the historian George Litvan. 'Only with real cooperation or confederation of these peoples can the national problems find a lasting solution.' That in turn may depend on the generosity and understanding of the West.

EAST GERMANY
The dream that bled to death

17 June 1953	Food shortages lead to uprising, put down by Soviet troops.
13 August 1961	Berlin Wall built to prevent exodus of citizens to the West.
Summer 1989	East Germans travel to Hungary, seeking to escape to the West through Austria.
11 September 1989	Hungary announces that it will not prevent them leaving for the West.
2 October 1989	20,000 people march in Leipzig in the biggest demonstration since 1953.
7 October 1989	Mikhail Gorbachov arrives for visit: urges reform on Politburo.
9 October 1989	70,000 demonstrate in Leipzig; security forces do not intervene.
18 October 1989	Erich Honecker quits: Egon Krenz appointed.
7 November 1989	Government resigns, Politburo follows; Hans Modrow appointed Prime Minister.
8–9 November 1989	Berlin Wall reopened; thousands cross in weekend of celebration.
6 December 1989	Egon Krenz forced to resign.
18 March 1990	Free elections.

'A revolution is of no value unless it is able to defend itself.' Lenin's words, writ large on the wall of secret police headquarters in Leipzig, brought smiles to the faces of many of the honest citizens who occupied the building late in November as East Germany's Communist regime went into its death throes.

The old men who had fought the good fight against Hitler in the 1930s had defended themselves for 40 years with an iron fist and the ever-present threat of violence. But they were powerless to defend themselves against their own people once the Berlin Wall was opened and the light shone in.

For the front-line state of the Warsaw Pact, the end came, in a sense, in the middle: from the moment that the wall was breached and the masses of East Germany saw West Germany – and saw that it worked – the outcome was never in doubt. Unification, in some shape or form, was only a matter of time. That much was clear weeks before the Prime Minister, Hans Modrow, spoke the words that no-one had expected to hear from the lips of a Communist leader: 'Deutschland, einig vaterland' – Germany, one fatherland.

The German Democratic Republic came into being in 1949, at an early peak in the Cold War. Berlin, the old German capital, found itself marooned 88 miles inside East Germany and divided among the wartime allies – the Soviet Union, the United States, France and Britain. It was not until 12 years later that Berlin itself was split into two distinct sectors and riven by a wall that was to stand for 28 years, two months and 27 days as the supreme symbol of the division of Europe.

When it happened, it happened without the slightest warning. The people of the Soviet sector of Berlin were astonished to awake on the morning of 13 August 1961 to find themselves cut off from the rest of the city by fat coils of barbed wire. Western nations were equally astonished when the East German news agency, ADN, began coughing out its historic dispatch: 'The present traffic situation on the borders of West Berlin is being used by ruling circles in West Germany and the intelligence agencies of Nato countries to undermine the economy of the German Democratic Republic.

'Through deceit, bribery and blackmail, West German Government bodies and military interests are inducing certain unstable elements in the German Democratic Republic to leave for West Germany. In the face of the aggressive aspirations of the reactionary forces of West Germany and the Nato allies, Warsaw Pact member states must take the necessary steps to guarantee the security of the GDR.' By erecting, in other words, a wall around it.

Although the Cold War was then at its height and East Germany's economy was haemorrhaging through the hole in Berlin's heart, no one had foreseen the construction of a physical barrier in the twentieth century. In the US, President John F. Kennedy lambasted the aide who brought him the news: 'Why in hell didn't we know about it?' he thundered. 'What can the military do?' The answer was precious little but wait and see.

In the early hours, the rolls of barbed wire were low enough for a man to jump over. Some did. Others, unable to believe the evidence of their eyes, stood and watched as the wire grew higher and higher and finally, on 17 August, began to be cast in concrete. By the time the wall came tumbling down, it was nine feet high. It ran 28 miles across the city and 70 miles around. It was fortified with hundreds of watchtowers and gun emplacements and was accompanied by a 20-foot-wide 'death strip' patrolled by dogs and peppered with machine gun traps.

When Berlin was first divided, the buildings along the new border afforded the only windows left open to the West. Many jumped from them – some to their deaths. When the windows were bricked up, they turned to the death strip, tunnelling underneath and sprinting across in a macabre dance that by 1989 had cost 75 people their lives.

In the language of totalitarianism, the wall was East Germany's 'fascist protective barrier'. In reality, however, it was designed to protect East Germany against the threat from within – to halt a wave of emigration to the West that was threatening not only the workplace but the very stability of the Communist regime. More than 2.7 million people had turned their backs on the republic since 1949 – 30,000 of them in the month before the wall went up. Escape was becoming an obsession. The escape hatch was the military regime that allowed free access among Berlin's four zones.

The wall was also meant to solve the problem of West Berlin's abuse of East Berlin's subsidized prices and cheap communal services. With the wall in place, East Berlin's already limited supply of consumer products was available exclusively to its own citizens. In the early days, the regime was to make much of this.

By 1989, despite being Comecon's most advanced economy, East Germany was a cruel reflection of its Siamese twin across the wall. Its cities were increasingly unlovely places of still-unrepaired war damage, soulless socialist tower blocks and belching, lurching two-stroke engines. Its villages were quiet, forgotten places that seemed frozen in time, waiting to be woken from a stupified sleep. Even in East Berlin, privileged over other cities as the country's leaders were privileged over other citizens, roads were in such poor repair that stopping at a red light was an experience akin to driving over unmade rubble. Thus, too, was the country running down – with a series of jolts to its backbone.

Although East Germany could boast of being a member of the world's industrial top 12, with the highest standard of living in Eastern

Europe and shops better stocked than in almost any other country of the Warsaw Pact, the East German 'miracle' was running out of steam. As an aide to Mikhail Gorbachov was to say later, it was an economy 'built on years of lying', on the crippling burden of subsidies that kept the prices of basic consumer goods at their 1950s' level and on subsidies from West Germany that only postponed the day of reckoning.

In an economy once held up as a shining example of socialist success, where central planning worked as well as it was ever likely to, productivity was declining and exports losing their competitive edge to Asian markets and Western technology. The boast of the 1970s – that East Germany was to the East bloc what West Germany was to the European Community – was no longer altogether true: after rapid growth in the first half of the 1980s, foreign trade stagnated in the second half as even the Soviet Union began to look elsewhere for better value. Nobody was starving, nobody was poor as the peasants of Romania were poor. But it took several years to get a telephone or hire a builder, and more than 10 years to acquire even a boxy, bumping, two-stroke Trabant that would not pass a pollution test anywhere in the West. The best shopping could be done only in the hard currency shops where the vast majority of East Germans, because of their unconvertible currency, could only window-shop.

The environment was one of the most polluted in the world – so bad that publication of the pollution figures was banned at the beginning of the 1980s. When the dam broke in 1989 and East German journalism took on a new, investigative life with all the hunger of a starving child, hospitals had sad, but surely not unexpected, tales of cancers, respiratory ailments, and eye and skin diseases – especially in the Leipzig and Lausitz regions where were concentrated most of the lignite mines that produced 70 percent of the country's electricity supply.

Five million tons of sulphur dioxide were being spewed into the atmosphere every year – 163,000 of them across the border to West Germany. So bad was the pollution spilling over into West Berlin that driving was restricted during red alerts. West Berliners, already losing patience with the crowds from across the wall, were therefore far from enchanted when the restrictions were suspended after the wall was opened to accommodate the millions of East Germans who chugged over in their two-stroke motors.

The state of the country's rather limited water resources was almost as bad, largely because of an intensive and, by socialist standards, efficient collective farming system that depended on 50 million tons of artificial fertiliser a year. Thus by the time it reached Dresden the Elbe contained 20 substances available only on doctor's prescription, as well as 10 times the amount of mercury dumped in the Rhine by West German industry.

In addition, although East Germany had won international recognition, peaking on that day in 1987 when Erich Honecker was received in Bonn with almost all the honours traditionally accorded to a foreign head of state, it had failed to create a real sense of identity, of belonging. It was not just the indifference of the country's leaders to the air their citizens breathed and the water they drank. It was their stubborn refusal to adapt to the change that was going on all around them, most notably across the borders in Hungary and Poland.

At the beginning of 1989, East Germany was the most heavily policed state in Eastern Europe after Romania, the only one that required Party members to wear badges in their lapels. More and more East Germans were beginning to ask whether the ruling Socialist Unity Party, the SED, already conducting public life with the neurotic rigidity of Brezhnev's Russia, might not, in holding out against change, become just such a paranoid fortress as Romania.

Honecker, Party leader and head of state for the past 18 years, not only publicly rejected the model of *perestroika* but saw fit to censor it in the interest of insulating East Germany against Gorbachov. To this end, the German-language edition of the Soviet journal *Sputnik* was banned and a church newspaper forbidden to reprint an article from *Moscow News* on the ground that it would constitute 'interference in the affairs of another state'. Gorbachov's arrival for East Germany's fortieth anniversary celebrations was denied live coverage. The Party's chief ideologist, Kurt Hager, summed it all up when asked about the changes set in motion in Moscow. 'If your neighbour wallpapered his flat', he responded, 'would you feel the need to decorate yours?'

As morale dropped, the regime continued blindly on its way, declaring in mid-1989 that 'the GDR, in the fortieth year of its existence, presents itself as a modern socialist state on German soil with a stable political development, a highly dynamic economy and a continued improvement in performance in all fields of social life'. But none of this was apparent to the man in the street who saw West German television nightly and who enjoyed greater freedom of travel to the West thanks to Honecker's one major piece of liberalisation of the mid-1980s. The young, especially, were beginning to ask whether Communism could be reformed – or would simply have to be done away with.

The month of May was a turning point, providing new evidence of change without East Germany, and obdurate immobility within. Municipal elections that month were not only single-candidate elections, despite Moscow's suggestion that there be competing candidates, but were blatantly rigged. Confronted with clear signs of popular protest, the regime stood firm. Asked about the desirability of having competing candidates, a councillor in Leipzig retorted that East Germany began reforming long before the Soviet Union – and, anyhow, with a growth rate of four percent who needed change?

It was unfortunate, to say the least, that these words coincided with an official lowering of the growth rate from four to three percent, and that the elections coincided with Hungary's decision to begin dismantling the barbed wire along its border with Austria, opening the way for East Germans, for whom Hungary was a favourite holiday spot, to slip, illegally, across the open border. As growing numbers of East Germans voted with their feet, Hungary found itself torn between its new liberalisation policies and an old treaty with East Germany that bound both countries to stop the citizens of the other leaving for a third country without authorisation.

Hungary initially erred on the side of its old friends and tightened security along the border. But as the East Germans kept on coming, the Government organised camps for would-be *émigrés* both in Budapest, the capital, and at Lake Balaton, a prime resort. For more than a month, the Hungarian Government waited and hoped that the two Germanies would resolve the problem around the negotiating table. But in vain. Honecker continued to give proof that he was lost for ever in the clear divisions and simple battles of his formative years. 'I had the good fortune to join a shock brigade in 1931', he reminisced on a mid-summer visit to the Soviet Union, making not the slightest mention of the shock events of the 1980s. 'We will never forget that heroic time.'

Soon after returning from Moscow, the old man, now approaching his seventy-seventh birthday, went into hospital for what was far more than the gall bladder operation announced to the public. His regime began showing signs of paralysis and the offer of talks for which Hungary was waiting never came.

On 11 September, the momentous announcement came over the Hungarian news agency MTI: the 1969 treaty with East Germany was being 'temporarily suspended' because it was incompatible with Hungary's other international obligations – a reference to its adhesion to the United Nations' convention requiring free passage to refugees promised reception in a third country. The border was to be opened at midnight. Hungary, seeking full acceptance in the international community, had acceded to the wishes of West Germany.

Warsaw Pact countries were quick to protest. Romania accused West Germany of 'blatant interference in the internal affairs of the GDR'. East Berlin accused Hungary of 'a clear violation' of its treaty obligations – and for monetary gain. 'Pieces of silver for Hungary', charged ADN. But Poland, whose Communist monopoly had just collapsed, cautiously approved Hungary's decision and the Soviet Union held its peace, tacitly confirming Gorbachov's promise of non-interference in the affairs of Eastern Europe.

The iron curtain parted. In the vanguard came the Trabants and the Wartburgs loaded high and trailing a haze of East European exhaust. Behind came the footsoldiers, beating the charter buses to the tape by walking over the border loaded equally high. Once across the border, having walked the most important few yards of their life, some bent and kissed the tarmac. Others cheered and hugged each other. Many, many wept. All that was lacking was the strings of the Berlin Philharmonic rising triumphantly into the glorious crescendo of the last act of Fidelio. But these refugees were not the raggedy band of political prisoners who stumble from their dungeons into the light in Beethoven's opera. They were solid, well-dressed citizens who were turning their backs on families, homes and jobs to breathe free air.

Crossing the border from East Germany to Czechoslovakia was no problem. But crossing from Czechoslovakia to Hungary required an exit permit. Those who did not have one, or who were unable to obtain one, abandoned their cars on the Czech side of the border and went over on foot under cover of darkness – often helped by

sympathetic Czech guards. Others felt strongly enough to risk swimming across the Danube, where around a dozen, according to some reports, drowned.

The initial destination for most of these 'transients', as they became known, was Passau, a West German border town on the Danube where reception camps were set up, the opera season postponed and scores of beds packed into city hall. Job offers flowed in, and mountains of clothing that shrank rapidly as the number of refugees climbed into five figures – and kept on climbing. On arrival in their new homeland, the East Germans each received a passport, $125, unemployment and health benefits, low-interest loans, free meals and temporary lodgings. It was only later that difficulties arose. Some found that although there were no waiting lists for cars, saving up to buy one could take years. Others found that even if they could afford to rent or buy, West Germany too had a housing shortage.

But the overwhelming reaction to being in the West was unadulterated, unrestrained jubilation. 'What a Monday', exclaimed a newscaster on a local radio station. 'Boris Becker wins the US Open and lots of DDR citizens win the Hungarian Open.'

The Great Escape, as it inevitably became known, was the largest migration of East Germans to the West since the wall was built, a resounding vote of no-confidence in a fossilised gerontocracy. Heartened by the rush, thousands more sought refuge in West German embassies in Prague and Warsaw, fearing that increased oppression would be the only response available to the old men in charge of their fate. 'We thought', they said as they ran, jumped and climbed into the embassy compounds, 'that if we didn't get out now we never would'.

After long days of diplomatic impasse, the embassy refugees were finally allowed to head West, on special trains provided by the East German Government, on the condition that they passed through East Germany to be formally expelled for 'disloyalty'. Once again, Germany's past was being sent after it by rail. But the face-saving arrangement backfired. As the 'freedom trains', sealed shut since leaving Prague, passed through East Germany, thousands more tried to jump aboard, besieging railway stations and blocking railway lines. There was a three-hour riot in Dresden when police using water cannon and batons attempted to drive back 15,000 people shouting: 'We want to leave'.

New refugees packed into the empty West German compounds. Confronted with an embarrassingly telegenic vote of no-confidence less than a week before its fortieth anniversary celebrations, East Germany demanded that the new refugees be thrown out and accused Bonn of breaking a promise that the mass evacuation would be a one-off operation. Bonn said there had been no such promise. It could not erect 'psychological barriers' around its embassies.

In a new bid to stop the exodus, East Germany on 3 October banned visa-free travel to all neighbouring states, effectively erecting a new wall that kept it apart from other Communist regimes. Now there was nowhere, even in Eastern Europe, that East Germans could visit without permission. The ban was announced as a 'temporary measure'. It was to last a bare month, overtaken by a pace of change that no-one, not even the most optimistic, had dared dream of.

When Gorbachov arrived in East Germany for the fortieth anniversary celebrations of 7 October, he found not a country 'moving forwards to strengthen socialism', as Honecker had written from his sickbed a month earlier, but a country deep in crisis. Job vacancies posted outside factories in East Berlin, Leipzig, Rostok and Jena were painful illustrations of the damage caused by the still-unstemmed exodus. Production targets were threatened, building sites brought to a halt, transport services in some areas scaled down, and restaurants and hospital departments closed. It was not only the writer Stephan Heym who foresaw that the Great Escape 'threatens to destroy the German Democratic Republic'.

On top of this, a small but vociferous opposition movement was beginning to come out from under the wings of the Protestant Church, a Church impelled by a sense of guilt at not having spoken out against Hitler in time. The largest of these groups, New Forum, was at first little more than a handful of disenchanted intellectuals who aimed only to encourage dialogue between the regime and its critics. It sought freer travel, freedom of speech and assembly, and amnesty for political prisoners. It wanted reform, but reform in a socialist framework. It grew fast – but was overtaken equally fast.

The Church was also the jumping-off point for the first regular public protests seen in East Germany in 40 years. The place was Leipzig. An industrial city quite literally choking to death from neglect, Leipzig had seen a sixth of its population desert it, mostly for other parts of the GDR, in the past five years. Outside the city centre, shops were closed, houses derelict and roads pitted with potholes. It had a strong, Church-based opposition movement, a thriving university and a comparatively low standard of living. Karl Marx Square in front of the city hall was about to become for East Germany what Wenceslas Square was to become for Czechoslovakia.

There had been quasi-political meetings in Leipzig's Nikolaikirche (St Nicholas Church) ever since 1987, 'peace discussions' attended by only a few hundred people and, ironically, encouraged by Honecker who had never been happy at the basing in East Germany of Soviet short-range missiles, deployed in response to Nato's cruise and Pershing-2 rockets. He was happy to see people demonstrating gently for peace, if the message was addressed to Moscow and to Nato. But the crowd grew rapidly and found a different purpose in September and October as the regime put its head in the sand and Honecker made it increasingly clear that while he was following *perestroika* 'with interest', he would not be following suit.

On 18 September, police and plainclothes men detained more than 100 protestors at one such meeting. The police trucks carrying those arrested away later drove straight into the crowd, injuring many. It was the beginning of a short-lived attempt to stifle the opposition by force.

On 2 October, within days of Gorbachov's arrival, more than 20,000 people gathered outside St Nicholas in the biggest demonstration since the 1953 uprising. They marched in procession towards Karl Marx Square, where they found their path blocked by police. In panic, some fled: others sought refuge in a nearby church, St Thomas (where Johann Sebastian Bach is buried), and set up a chant of 'Gorby, Gorby'. Police moved in and broke the demonstration up with force. In Dresden, demonstrators were dispersed with water cannon on three consecutive nights.

Into this growing unrest, on what was to have been 'Honi's' crowning moment, flew the Soviet leader and his wife Raisa. The regime that had invited them was showing clear signs of *perestroika* anxiety: East German television did not transmit the couple's arrival at Schonefield Airport and did not publish the schedule for the visit. Not unsurprisingly, the crowds that turned out to greet the Gorbachovs were thin on the ground. Gorbachov, like his policies before him, was being censored.

Gorbachov urged patience. 'Don't panic', he told East Berliners. 'Don't be depressed. We'll go on together fighting for socialism.' But his real message was for Honecker. Speaking publicly, he said: 'I think that dangers exist only for those who don't grasp the situation, who don't react to life'. Speaking privately, he told the old man: 'Those who delay are punished by life itself'. Honecker's response was typically obdurate. 'Those who are declared dead', he said, 'usually live a long time.' It was one of the last occasions on which Honecker was able to show publicly how little he understood of the new world about him. Ten days later, on 18 October, he was politically dead, citing ill-health after 18 years as party leader and head of state.

Within an hour of Gorbachov's departure, anti-Government demonstrations broke out in many parts of the country. In East Berlin, police and militia with dogs, sticks and water cannon attacked a candle-lit march outside Gethsemane Church, a neo-Gothic pile known in official circles as 'the rebel church'. At no time did the crowd show violence, although it did show fear.

'Please tell me we will win', a frail old woman whispered to a Western journalist as the police advanced, kicking and beating anyone who attempted to avoid arrest. By the end of the day, two of the city's prisons were filled with protestors and at least 100 people were injured. There were similar protests in Leipzig, Dresden, Karl Marx Stadt, Potsdam and Halle.

But Honecker's fate was sealed on 9 October, just two days after the celebrations he had meant to be glorious, when 70,000 people poured into the streets of Leipzig for the now-regular Monday demonstration. The huge crowd moved slowly, uncertainly, fully expecting to be stopped by police, hope in its heart but fear in its stomach. Motorists hooted their horns as the mass advanced with only a few hastily scrawled banners with simple words like 'Freedom' on them and occasional shouts of 'Give peace a chance'. Local party officials, including Kurt Masur, the conductor of Leipzig's Gewandhaus Orchestra, joined an appeal read over loudspeakers for 'essential change'.

Lorryloads of police with full riot gear and live ammunition were parked in every side street. The Kampfgruppe – the people's militia – were lined up and ready to go. Hospitals had been told to have empty beds. Extra blood supplies and doctors had been sent from Berlin. But the troops were not ordered to intervene. It was a tacit admission that force, Honecker's main weapon, could not win this war and might even be counter-productive. From that day on, the floodgates were open. The demonstrations, and the pressure, grew.

In East Berlin, rock musicians, jazz groups and solo guitarists performed a 'concerto against violence'. The officially approved Writers' Union called for 'revolutionary reforms', insisting that 'what must be feared is not reform, but fear of reform'. Herman Kant, President of the union and a member of the Party's Central Committee, wrote an open letter urging self-criticism. The Communist youth paper, *Junge Welt*, took a giant step by printing it.

Stephen Hemelling, an old friend of Honecker and one of East Germany's best-known approved authors, urged Honecker to 'grasp the nettle, even if we do not like the individuals involved, or as Communists feel ill at ease with some of their ideas'. The Mayors of Dresden and Leipzig called for dialogue. The Politburo, formally acknowledging the magnitude of the crisis facing it, issued a statement calling for 'cooperation based on trust' between the Party and the people, for 'a more comprehensive use ... of the forums of social democracy'.

As the pressure on Honecker grew, a formula was found to allow East Germans awaiting passage to the West in other Warsaw Pact countries to renounce their citizenship and leave quietly. But it was not enough. On 16 October, as the Politburo met in emergency session, more than 100,000 people took to the streets in Leipzig, winning their first mention in the state-controlled media. At the end of two days' deliberation, Honecker, still trapped in his memories of the struggle that in 1945 seemed so miraculously to have succeeded, finally acknowledged that his time was over – his life's work, in effect, an illusion. With him went the two other most powerful men in the country – Gunther Mittag, East Germany's economic czar, and Joachim Hermann, its propaganda chief.

A West German newspaper, *Bild Zeitung*, later gave details of Honecker's last stand, quoting a member of the Central Committee. It said Gorbachov had told East German leaders he did not believe Honecker's health was good enough for him to continue running the country. After Gorbachov's departure, a Politburo meeting was called at which Honecker insisted that 'everything will collapse if we give an inch'. But others in the Politburo responded that the demonstrations would, if ignored, turn into an uprising – and the Soviet Union would not intervene this time, despite its 380,000 troops. Honecker threatened to resign all his posts and, on getting no support, left the room – 'an old and broken man'.

But the old regime's rearguard action was not over. As Hungary officially shed its Stalinist past after more than 40 years of one-party rule by approving a new, Western-style constitution, into Honecker's shoes stepped 'grinning Egon' Krenz, a longtime Honecker protégé who only three weeks earlier had travelled to China to applaud the brutal crushing of the democracy movement. He was to last 47 days, fooling nobody with his sudden predilection for walkabouts and television chats and a conveniently modest new home in suburban Pankow.

A tailor's son and former teacher, the 52-year-old Krenz was the youngest member of the old Politburo but already had a reputation as an entrenched hardliner. Like Honecker, he had headed the Free German Youth and as the Politburo member responsible for internal security had been in charge of the Stasi, the hated, pervasive secret police. His manner could be convivial, but that was widely attributed to the amount of alcohol he drank.

Krenz's true colours showed very clearly in the first speech he made as the new face of East Germany, on the day of his appointment. He promised *wende* – a change of direction – but not a change in the leading role of the Party. He pledged to open a dialogue, but made no promise to include in it the fledgling opposition. What he did promise, ominously, was to restore 'law and order' in answer to those who 'abused social democracy'.

Even East Germany's rubber stamp Parliament was not fully convinced. When Krenz's appointment came up for confirmation on 24 October, 26 deputies voted against him and another 26 abstained. All 52 belonged to the four-party 'national bloc' that had previously been nothing but a Communist Party puppet, allowed to contribute a few candidates to the single-candidate election lists but not permitted an independent political identity. Outside Parliament, a small crowd chanted 'Nobody asked us' and 'Reform now'. The Great Escape continued unabated, with a record number of more than 2000 people transiting through Hungary on Krenz's first full day in office. In the days that followed, Krenz not only showed that he was resistant to anything more than relatively superficial change – an amnesty for political prisoners, limited liberalisation of travel laws – but also, more fundamentally, that he too still belonged in the past. On an official visit to Moscow at the beginning of November, he said he had 'no regrets' over the past; much had been accomplished. The roads taken by Hungary and Poland were not the roads for him. 'I don't like models or standards.' He was ready to 'consider and examine all ideas that emerge', but not necessarily to implement them.

What was said behind the scenes in Moscow is not recorded, but it is clear that there was tough talking. Immediately upon his return to Berlin, Krenz sacked the Party's powerful union boss, Harry Tisch, and Honecker's wife Margot, a woman who had totally redesigned the country's education system since taking it over in 1963: in the Gorbachov era, kindergarten children in East Germany were taking lessons in 'anti-fascist indoctrination'. On 7 November, the Government of Willi Stoph, Prime Minister on and off since 1964, resigned, followed within 24 hours by the entire Politburo. Twelve old Stalinists, including 81-year-old General Erich Mielke, longtime Minister for State Security, were consigned to the dustbin of history, replaced by a roughly equal mixture of hardliners and less-hardliners.

Stoph's replacement was 61-year-old Hans Modrow, a reform-minded economist who was disliked by Honecker and had been consigned to 16 years of provincial exile as Party chief of Dresden. It was a popular choice, but nothing, it seemed, could restore confidence in the country while Krenz remained at the helm – not even his decision to lift the restriction on emigration through Czechoslovakia.

In the middle of the biggest leadership shake-up since 1949, a million marchers filled East Berlin's Alexanderplatz to speak their mind about the new regime. Krenz came in for special attack. Posters depicted him as a devil, as the wolf in Little Red Riding Hood and as 'Krenz Xiao Ping' an embarrassing reminder of his support for the brutal attack in Tiananmen Square.

On the country's borders, the Great Escape continued. Thousands headed for the little town of Pomezi on the border between Czechoslovakia and West Germany, at a point where the two Germanies were separated by only a few miles, to take advantage of the new free passage through Czechoslovakia. Thousands more headed for the re-opened West German Embassy in Prague, and in Hungary they continued crossing to the West at a rate of 400 a day. By the time the Berlin Wall was opened, some 225,000 people in a population of only 16.7 million had left the country for good since the start of the year – most of them between the ages of 20 and 40. And so it was that the wall came down for exactly the same reason that it went up: to keep East Germans in East Germany.

West Berliners of all ages welcomed millions of East Berliners as the wall came down on 8–9 November 1989. (Photo: Bill Robinson)

It fell to the Party boss of East Berlin, Gunther Schabowski, to announce at a news conference on the afternoon of 8 November that, starting the following day, East Germans would be free to leave at any point on the borders without special permission, for one minute, one month or for the rest of their lives. In the middle of reading from a printed statement, Schabowski faltered as if unable to believe what he saw before him. East European diplomats said later they had been told that a line scheduling the opening for the morning of the following day had been dropped in transcription: Schabowski knew it, but was unable to do anything about it.

As midnight approached, with border police clearly not ready for it, the wall became the focus of the biggest street party in European history, a combination, one of those present wrote, of the fall of the Bastille and a New Year's Eve blowout. Men, women and children, old and young, strong and weak, poured into the streets, many of them with bottles of champagne and party hats, shouting, as the countdown ended: 'Tor auf, tor auf' – 'Open the gate'.

On the stroke of twelve, both sides of Berlin erupted. Laughing, crying, shouting and singing, the crowds poured through the crossings and, where they were packed tight, climbed up and over the wall. As morning dawned, the Ku'damm, West Berlin's glitzy main street, was transformed by tens of thousands of poor relations from the East, wide-eyed as little children. Some West Germans offered precious West German marks to buy coffee and beer; others made a quick buck by hawking gilt as gold and cheap beads as precious stones. All that glistered seemed, that day, to be gold.

Moscow called the opening of the borders 'wise' and 'positive' but lost no time in warning that reunification should not even be considered before the dissolution of Nato and the Warsaw Pact. In Bonn, members of the Bundestag rose to their feet and sang the national anthem, some of them with tears in their eyes. Chancellor Helmut Kohl interrupted an official visit to Poland to join the celebrations, declaring, despite Moscow's warning, that 'unity will eventually be achieved. The wheel of history is turning faster'. In America, President Bush said only that he was 'very happy' – perhaps

A West Berliner takes a hammer to the wall close to the Brandenburg Gate.
(Photo: Bill Robinson)

worried that the wheel was turning so fast his friend Gorbachov would be thrown clear off.

The party, the largest movement of European population ever recorded in one day, continued well past the weekend as millions of East Germans made the pilgrimage west – two million of them in the first 48 hours. Cities like East Berlin, Potsdam and even faraway Erfurt turned into ghost towns as West Berlin exerted its magnetic pull. New crossing points were opened and a long-closed underground station re-opened, but nothing could relieve the crush. At one crossing point, Helmstedt, the line of cars stretched for 30 miles and reaching the border took all day.

Completely overcome, West Berlin eventually halted all bus traffic and closed a number of underground stations. The Mayor, Walter Momper, appealed to Berliners to stop climbing the wall after East German guards at the Brandenburg Gate, one of the last gates to open, used water cannon to hose hundreds off. Deprived of one route across the wall, the crowds knocked a section down; East German guards propped it back up.

In the days that followed, East Berliners painted their side of the wall in a mirror image of the western side, covering it with graffiti and scores of hopping rabbits, the only creatures that had flourished in the death strip. But it was still early days, and the wall's guards had not received orders about painting, so they whitewashed it over, imperfectly hiding the explosion of energy beneath. One old lady returned immediately to the attack, hollering as a guard grabbed her from behind: 'Didn't you notice that the balance of power has changed?' Others contented themselves with decorating the slabs that had been cut out to make new gates. 'The wall', they wrote, 'belongs to the people. We will continue painting.'

With the opening of the wall and a series of reformist manoeuvres that constituted, in the Party's terms, a revolution, Krenz bought himself a little time. He instituted a dialogue with factory workers, promised that Parliament would in future be more than a rubber stamp, relaxed the restrictions on the media and gave the green light to unofficial talks with groups like New Forum. But the changes were only fuel to the fire of popular protest as daily revelations by the media made increasingly clear that the elite had preached water while drinking wine. Demands for radical reform grew as the public evaluated present change in the light of past abuse.

On 18 November, Modrow, a priceless asset for the Communists as they struggled to recover from Honecker's disgrace, presented his new cabinet, in which non-Communist parties from the national bloc held 11 of 28 portfolios. At the same time, Modrow announced his plan for a new East Germany – 'a socialist state', he said, 'and a sovereign German state'. He proposed a more market-oriented

West Berliners use the curving stretch of wall around the Brandenburg Gate as a grandstand. (Photo: Bill Robinson)

economy, 'no planning without the market but no unplanned market economy', open to cooperation with the West; a 'cooperative relationship' with the European Community; a streamlined bureaucracy and a reformed education system; legal reforms, individual liberties and a Constitutional Court to check the power of the state; a 'new level' of relationship with West Germany, but no 'dangerous speculation about reunification'.

Parliament, which had already begun to flex its democratic muscles by electing a non-Communist, Gunther Maleuda of the Democratic Farmers' Party, as Speaker, approved the package unanimously – and returned its attention to the all-consuming business of investigating corruption under the Stalinist old guard.

The evidence of corruption that emerged in these days astonished everyone, including Western diplomats who had George Orwell drummed into them at school. 'That they were corrupt one knew', said a senior West German diplomat who heard about the Politburo's luxury compound at Wandlitz, north of Berlin, from the West German technicians called in to repair the West German satellite dishes, videos and other gadgets. 'But one tended to differentiate between them. There seemed to be some honest men, but apparently not. They all had the Tartar attitude of exploitation: settle with your cattle, eat everything and when there is nothing left, move on.'

As the days went by, it became clear that Wandlitz was only the tip of the iceberg. There were also the weekend hunting lodges, the holiday homes and even holiday islands, and such little perks as the £13 million 'sanatorium' of Harry Tisch's trade union federation – a five-star pick-me-up equipped with everything necessary for the health of the elite from bars and barbecues to double bathrooms.

With these images filling the television screens, other confessions went almost unnoticed: that football matches had been consistently rigged in favour of General Mielke's team, Dynamo Berlin; that museum pieces were sold to the West; even ancient cobblestones ripped up and shipped off for personal profit. It was even reported that Honecker had been involved in the cocaine trade. Nobody denied it and nobody, by the same token, seemed surprised. 'Drugs, arms, what's the difference?' asked a Western diplomat. 'Both kill.'

But the most shocking revelations for ordinary citizens burdened with their unconvertible East Marks were the foreign currency fortunes built up by the likes of Alexander Schalck-Golodkowski, the former Secretary of State in the Economy Ministry who, together with his deputy Manfred Siedel, was accused of siphoning £72 million out of the country – much of it from arms sales to the Third World.

As their former leaders were shown to have feet of clay and bath-taps of gold, people who had been afraid to talk even privately to friends suddenly felt free to talk to almost anyone. Political prisoners spoke of torture, of the inhuman, rat-like conditions of 'transit trains', of being forced to handle chemical waste with bare hands, of daily humiliation and degradation. Women in a village near Karl Marx

Souvenir hunters on the West Berlin side attacked the wall with all the frustration of 28 years of isolation. (Photo: Bill Robinson)

Stadt recounted how the Stasi had locked them into their factory when they attempted to organise a strike only a month earlier, and then had stripped them naked. Villagers in Wolletz, a lakeside village east of Berlin, told how the Stasi threw them out of their homes, wanting them for themselves.

Faced with this avalanche of evidence – 'A sea of mud stretching before us', was how the Peasants' Party paper, the *Bauern Echo*, put it – the new Politburo resigned, with Krenz at its head, on 3 December. The Party was looking decidedly pale; only two days earlier, Parliament had voted overwhelmingly to end its monopoly of power, to remove its vanguard role from the Constitution. Little more than four weeks after Krenz had pledged to fight such a development, the once all-powerful Party was leaderless, temporarily in the hands of a working committee effectively headed by a young lawyer who had been prominent in human rights' cases, Gregor Gysi.

The Politburo's collapse began a chain reaction. The Stasi leadership resigned collectively, as did the District Council of Rostock, the centre, *inter alia*, of Schalck-Golodkowski's arms operation. Several local officials committed suicide. Membership in the party that had once been one of Eastern Europe's largest ruling parties, with an eighth of the population enrolled, skydived as more than 500,000 of 2.3 million members burnt, tore up or handed in their Party cards.

For the older generation of Communists, it was the collapse of a lifetime, an experience so bitter they had trouble putting words to it. 'Oh, we knew it was wrong how they lived', said Paula Kleinmann, a 51-year-old veteran of the Party, who as a young woman had been imprisoned by the Nazis, 'and we grumbled in small groups at home. But we didn't know it was so bad. I am sad, sad, sad . . . but if I didn't strangle myself as a young girl in prison, I will overcome this. Our Erich believed that our young people nowadays want the same as before; to demonstrate, to sing was our weapon. But they don't. We never managed to get youth on our side and now we have nothing to offer.'

For old Communists such as Mrs Kleinmann, the shock of the Party's collapse was compounded by the legal action taken against the old guard once Parliament removed their immunity from prosecution. The first to see a warrant were Mittag and Tisch, accused of having squandered public property and done 'serious damage to the economy'. At the same time, 12 of the old guard, including Honecker, were expelled from the Party. Much, much more was to follow and not everyone welcomed it. A Polish diplomat shared Mrs Kleinmann's fears of a witchhunt, saying: 'I can't imagine a handful of men ruining East Germany to this extent. It is wrong to arrest them. We didn't do this even in Poland. It wasn't them; it was the system.'

East Berliners in a Trabant, the smoky two-stroke museum piece that symbolises East Germany's decline, are welcomed to the West. (Photo: Bill Robinson)

Until this time, the mood inside East Germany had been one of tremendous excitement, of awakening. Time not spent on debate and discussion was considered wasted. The leaders of New Forum were unable to stop yawning. 'We haven't slept for nights . . .' There were nightly meetings in the churches; consultation centres, telephone contact numbers, new independent professional organisations springing up daily. Almost overnight, it seemed, the impossible had become possible; the undreamed of, reality.

'Nobody is afraid any more', said Dr Harald Mau, founder of a free association of doctors and dentists. 'Today I can say: "You're a secret policeman. Go. Shut up."' A border guard who only weeks earlier had orders to shoot to kill chuckled over the regime he had served all his life: 'I used to say to my wife: "Where's the boring party paper so I can go to sleep?" I used the paper for only two things – my bird and my cabbage. Now I read it.' In bars and restaurants, formerly surly waiters began to smile – knowing that there would be change, and, if there was not, that they would be able to demand it.

But then the mood turned sour. The oranges, bananas and videos suddenly flooding the market fooled nobody. There were attacks on Stasi offices. Ugly-sounding 'citizens' councils' and 'vigilance groups' were formed across the country. In East Berlin, more than one Western diplomat found his Mercedes brought to a halt by angry young men smelling privilege. In the countryside, state guest houses were put under lock and seal, Honecker's country estate was raided and hunting lodges stormed.

Catching up on 40 years of frustration and fury, an East Berlin woman roundly abuses the long-hated East Berlin border guards. (Photo: Bill Robinson)

Until the border was opened, most East Germans had thought of East Berlin as seventh heaven. Having seen the splendour that was West Berlin, they suddenly wanted to hang their district secretary from the nearest sour apple tree. Appalled, the working committee appealed for calm and warned against chaos and anarchy. Opposition groups called for elections, no later than May, to prevent further disintegration. The appeals were not heeded.

Factories were threatened with violence if they dared to employ former Party functionaries or old members of the security services. Mob justice began to raise a threatening head, beginning, surprisingly, in Dresden, where a man was yanked from his car, called a 'Communist swine' and threatened with lynching with his own tow rope.

The question of reunification aroused especially strong emotions, with shouts of 'Nazis out' answering cries of 'We are one people' at the Leipzig rallies. Heym spoke for many when he said he feared that the democratic dream could turn into a nightmare. He had seen faces 'filled with hatred' at demonstrations and could not but remember the months that preceded Hitler's rise to power.

As the tumult grew, groups like New Forum began to find themselves on the wrong side of the tracks, urging restraint where the crowd wanted resolve, and caution where the crowd wanted action. The opposition, for the most part, wanted to maintain a separate East German identity – valuing the asceticism, strong community and rock-like faith of East Germany over the materialistic hustle and bustle of West Germany – and to refloat the Communist Party, not to sink it. But the mass of the people seemed to want a complete break with the past – and unification with West Germany if that was what it took to obtain the standard of living they had glimpsed across the wall. Unlike Czechoslovakia, blessed with a Vaclav Havel, or Poland, with a Lech Walesa, East Germany had no charismatic opposition leaders. Anyone who came even remotely close was arrested and shipped across the border, to West German exile and East German oblivion. Instead there were gentle, soft-spoken folk who, from the comfort of their book-lined studies and cosy salons, preached arrogantly of the dangers of structures, of parties and party leaders.

At a typical meeting late in October the co-founders of New Forum – Barbel Bohley, a painter, and Jens Reich, a molecular biologist – showed how very far they were from the man in the street. 'Give Krenz a chance', they suggested. 'And definitely no to unification. We don't want to be an appendage to West Germany.'

Nor was the diminuitive Gregor Gysi, elected to replace Krenz at an emergency Party Congress in December, the man to fire the imagination of the public and in so doing save the Communists from final collapse. Under his direction, the key congress did little more than make its name twice as long – the Socialist Unity Party–Party of Democratic Socialism – and thus, its critics said waggishly, twice as forgettable. It just as quickly dropped the first half, as if by changing its name it could obliterate its past.

The Gysi the public saw at the congress was a consummate showman, but not a strategist; a cautious reformer perhaps, but not a magician. He stripped away the old – expelling an outraged Krenz and 13 other former officials – but seemed to have no vision of the future except through a utopian, ill-defined 'third way'. Nor could he get rid of the ghost of the dying Honecker, a pathetic, even tragic figure as he was thrown from his Wandlitz home, charged with treason, corruption and misuse of office, jailed, released and finally admitted to a Church-run home for the handicapped to await trial. The old man had, in his day, been a reasonably successful, reasonably benevolent leader by East European standards. But it was not a time when charity was abroad in East Germany – even for a confused cancer-stricken septuagenarian able to believe he had made mistakes but not to believe that everything he had stood for had been wrong.

The man many hoped would succeed in giving East German Communism a human face, and a new lease of life, was the Prime Minister, Hans Modrow. But this too was not to be, however much Modrow had distinguished himself from other party notables.

The son of working class parents, Modrow had maintained a modest lifestyle throughout his 16 years in Dresden. He eschewed special Party shops in favour of his local supermarket, swam at the public baths and inhabited an ordinary, four-room flat. It was a unique style he carried over to high office in Berlin, walking to work with briefcase in hand and missing his first news conference in order not to miss his mother's birthday.

Outlining his plan for a new East Germany, Modrow stressed his 'clear rejection' of Communist interference, especially to the detriment of the economy. He pledged 'openness and honesty, orderliness and lawful behaviour, modesty and economy and confident professionalism in place of slogans and glib words'. He was in favour of a 'pan-European Economic Area' and would seek a 'new level' of relationship with West Germany. But certainly not unity; East Germany must find new legitimacy as 'a socialist state and a sovereign German state'.

Despite setting a date for free elections – May 1990 – Modrow failed to live up to the moment. In resisting real change, he fuelled fears that the Communists would not loosen their grip on power and so contributed to the growing unrest that exploded, in January, into an attack on Stasi headquarters in Berlin and into violence between supporters and opponents of unification in Leipzig.

Misjudging the popular mood, Modrow insisted on an early replacement for the despised Stasi, citing a wave of neo-Nazi attacks that, whether or not they were contrived as many believed, undoubtedly permitted Gysi, in his pre-electoral period, to cry: 'We are and always have been the only party dedicated to the anti-fascist struggle'. The opposition complained that round table talks with the Government were becoming increasingly arid and the answers to their questions increasingly evasive. Talk of state control deepened fear for the economic future.

Only after New Forum threatened to organise a general strike, and the Christian Democrats withdrew from his coalition Government, did Modrow show real, if reactive, leadership. To appease fears of Communists clinging to power, he proposed to resign his Party membership until the elections were over. To prevent further administrative disintegration at a time when local governments were collapsing, resigning or simply throwing in the towel because of the animus against them, he brought the election date forward to 18 March and in the meantime invited the opposition into a 'government of national responsibility'.

Then, in February, he bowed to the prevailing wind and produced his own unification plan, tacitly acknowledging that to attempt to prolong East Germany's separate existence could be dangerous. Unveiled 48 hours after Modrow returned from talks with Gorbachov, the plan not only suggested that the Soviet leader was beginning to accept the inevitability of reunification, but also came reasonably close to the thinking of Chancellor Kohl. Both German leaders were now committed to step-by-step unity, but without a firm timetable. The only card left in Modrow's hand was to insist that a united Germany be a neutral Germany – an insistence immediately rejected by Nato Secretary General Manfred Woerner.

With East Germany apparently doomed to disappear off the map – by 1992 at the latest, Kohl said confidently, sensing an opportunity for personal political mileage – the elections were stripped of much of the excitement that free elections should have had. The majority wanted only higher wages and better benefits; the minority was already in mourning for the death of a nation; the election winner, as one of the new politicians put it, would have little to do but negotiate the terms of surrender.

The election race, such as it was, was already being surrendered. The Social Democrats were so closely linked to their West German namesakes that the SPD West was even printing their election posters. The Christian Democrats were forging ties with the ruling party in Bonn. The Leipzig-based German Social Union was linked to West Germany's Christian Social Union; the Free Democratic Party mirrored West Germany's. New Forum, resolutely East German, was way down in the polls, promising to get considerably less than 10 percent of the vote as the smallest of the new opposition groupings. 'They have hijacked our elections', Barbel Bohley said bitterly. But they had also hijacked New Forum: at its first national congress, the group had been riven by dissent – most especially over the unity question: those opposing unity, the majority only a few months earlier, were now the minority.

The influence of West Germany was spreading everywhere, like irrigation waters over reclaimed land. Joint commissions had already been established in a wide range of fields from economic cooperation and culture to posts and telecommunications. Joint patents had been issued for scientific cooperation. Joint ventures had been permitted on the condition of a controlling East German interest of 51 percent. On those terms, with unity apparently around the corner, there would be few takers.

Several weeks earlier, the History Museum in East Berlin had quietly locked up the section covering 1949–61, so erasing at a stroke an entire chapter of national history. Now the nation was preparing to erase itself. Not with the giddy jubilation with which it had walked across the wall on 9 November, perhaps, but almost. The Soviet Zone, like the Soviet empire, was racing into history.

BULGARIA
The Party calls the tune

May 1989	Ethnic Turks demonstrate against enforced assimilation; 60 killed.
June 1989	Huge exodus of ethnic Turks begins, in the biggest migration in Europe since World War II.
16 October 1989	Environment Conference under the auspices of CSCE opens in Sofia, providing cover for first legal opposition activity for 40 years.
24 October 1989	Petar Mladenov resigns creating a leadership crisis.
26 October 1989	40 environmental activists beaten and arrested.
3 November 1989	5000 environmentalists allowed to demonstrate peacefully.
10 November 1989	Todor Zhivkov, Bulgaria's leader for 35 years, ousted by Mladenov in Central Committee coup.
18 November 1989	More than 50,000 people demonstrate for democracy in Sofia.
11 December 1989	Communist Party proposes an end to its monopoly of power, and a multi-party system.
May or June 1990	Free elections to be held.

Of all Eastern Europe's revolutions, the one in Bulgaria is the strangest. Virtually everybody in the country, from the Communist Party down, admits that Bulgaria has been badly ruled for more than 40 years. Mismanagement, corruption and authoritarianism on a truly heroic scale have been exposed, and acknowledged. As one opposition politician, Alexander Chirkov, put it: 'Bulgaria could be a Garden of Eden, but 43 years ago we gave ourselves a goat as a gardener'. Yet when Bulgaria goes to the polls in May or June for its first free election in two generations, it is the goat – the Communist Party – which stands the best chance of winning.

Even by the standards of the Balkans, which do not invariably follow European patterns, this is a paradox that requires some explanation. Uniquely in Eastern Europe, the Communist Party in Bulgaria has managed to identify itself so closely with the changes that are taking place that it is able to take credit for them, instead of being blamed for the mess it has created. As in Romania, the removal of a hated figurehead has discharged much of the revolutionary fervour, leaving the Party as the only credible organ of government. That, and the curiosities of Bulgarian history, explain how the Party in Sofia has so far managed its remarkable feat of escapology.

Bulgaria today is moving steadily from a totalitarian Communist state to a multi-party democracy through a top-down transformation led by reform-minded Communists who are determined to stay in power. The country's opposition is much less experienced and more narrowly based than in most of the rest of Eastern Europe, which means that the Communist Party has been largely allowed to dictate the scope and pace of change.

The key moment was 10 November 1989, when Foreign Minister Petar Mladenov ousted old hardline leader Todor Zhivkov in a Central Committee coup, opening the door for the small oppressed dissident movement to step up its activities. Mladenov quickly replaced Zhivkov's supporters and policies with those closer to his own liking and kept one step ahead of the opposition both inside and outside the Party.

Bulgaria's Communist Party is probably the strongest and most popular in Eastern Europe. Mladenov and his supporters have skilfully adopted and sometimes even pre-empted opposition demands for political, economic and social progress, at time leaving the opposition apparently redundant. In a popularity poll in January 1990, leading Communists occupied many of the top positions – a far cry from the situation elsewhere in Eastern Europe.

The Bulgarian Communist Party, to which about 900,000 people out of a total population of nine million belong, never endured the traumas of its counterparts in Czechoslovakia and Hungary. There were no mass expulsions of liberal thinkers in the 1960s and 1970s, so the Bulgarian Party retained an inner capacity for renewal and renovation. Within a month of taking power from Zhivkov, the reformers proposed giving up the Party's constitutionally guaranteed right to a leading role in society; announced full multi-party elections within six months; and suggested separating Communist Party and state power. By the time of the Party Congress in February 1990, Zhivkov was under arrest for corruption, abuse of power and inciting ethnic hatred, together with his son-in-law, his son and closest adviser, and reform Communists had replaced the old guard in many key positions.

As a result of these moves and the weakness of the opposition the Communists are expected to emerge as at least the biggest party, even if they do not have an overall majority, in May or June after the country's first free elections for over 40 years. The Bulgarian opposition is weak because it has no recent national model of revolt around which to fashion a mass people's movement. Unlike the Central Europeans in the Soviet bloc, these cautious and suspicious Balkan people hardly dissented in the 1960s and 1970s, and there was no pro-democracy movement in the 1980s. Bulgaria's first dissident organisation, the Independent Society for Human Rights, was not founded until 16 January 1988 – and even they chose the twentieth anniversary of an event outside Bulgaria's borders, the suicide of the Czechoslovak student Jan Palach, as the day to establish themselves.

Bulgarians also lacked an independent trade union movement until Podkrepa (Support) was founded in February 1989. Initially this was an intellectuals' union, rejecting the use of strikes. Despite its rapid increase in membership and growing militancy, it has remained fairly ineffective. This is largely a consequence of the country's agricultural traditions. Before World War II, over 70 percent of the population worked on the land (compared to nine percent today) and a modern proletariat did not emerge until the 1960s, when Zhivkov undertook breakneck industrialisation.

The first generation that left the land harboured the peasant dream of becoming a citizen, which in Bulgaria was equivalent to becoming a worker. This, coupled with the Stalinist notion of the leading role of the working class, relegated intellectuals to second-class status, and encouraged a feeling of worker self-satisfaction. This largely explains why Bulgaria's democratic opposition is led by intellectuals with little support from industrial workers. In addition, the opposition faces a formidable enemy. The Communist Party controls a gigantic *nomenklatura* of 216,000 bureaucrats, who dominate every social, political and economic activity. This is proportionally far greater than in the other socialist bloc countries. These bureaucrats have a vested interest in maintaining the status quo and are still an obstacle even to Mladenov's plans.

With its mass membership, the Communist Party also supplements the work of the secret police with a wide network of informers. These people send anonymous 'signals' about their neighbours, workmates, friends and relatives at any sign of political or social deviance. Bulgaria's isolation at the south-eastern edge of Europe; its pro-Soviet leanings; and a people among whom less than one percent can speak a Western language, mean that its few brave dissidents have long been overshadowed and overlooked.

The country was dominated by Todor Zhivkov for 35 years. He was born to a peasant family and although a cunning and successful politician, he had neither great political depth nor particular intelligence. His successor, Petar Mladenov, described him as 'morbid, suspicious and having maniacal ambition'. Zhivkov was an apparatchik who, like Stalin, seized the elements of power. He rewrote his own and the country's histories and built an unaccountable and inaccessible personal fiefdom which loyally followed every twist and turn of Soviet policy until the arrival of Gorbachov.

Initially, Zhivkov embraced Gorbachov's ideas for *glasnost* and *perestroika* and in July 1987 issued his grandly entitled 'Keynotes of the Conception about the Further Construction of Socialism in Bulgaria' – July Conception for short. In fact, it was the work of the relatively liberally minded Central Committee Secretary for Ideology, Stoyan Mikhailov, who was removed from the leadership soon afterwards. At the time, Zhivkov's July Conception was more far-reaching than Gorbachov, but his mistake was to think that it would be enough to make sweeping statements and agree with the Soviet leader, as he had always done in the past. When he realised that Gorbachov actually intended to do what he said, Zhivkov began to backtrack and distance himself from the Soviet leader.

Zhivkov surrounded himself with nonentities, and anybody showing signs of intellectual rigour or challenge was pushed into a political dead end, or plagiarised and then dispensed with. This has created a shortage of talented leaders in Bulgaria. Zhivkov also benefitted from the absence of democratic experience upon which Bulgarians might otherwise have attempted to build a lasting tradition. In both world wars, Bulgaria took the German side, in a desperate search for a great power to sponsor its demands to reclaim territories lost to Serbia, Greece, Romania and Turkey before World War I.

Between the wars, Bulgarians did enjoy some open elections, but the political system was bedevilled by intrigue and violence. Finally, a coup introduced a Mussolini-style system, which banned political parties and independent trade unions, and purged the professions. Bulgaria was liberated from the Nazis in September 1944 by the Soviet Red Army. A broad-based Fatherland Front Government was then set up to establish a 'People's Democracy'. Elections followed, but by 1948 all opposition parties and opinion were outlawed as the Soviet bloc was Stalinised.

The Communist leadership maintained a cultural power base and established deep roots by appealing to the nation's highly developed sense of egalitarianism, and preference for social equality over market competition. This had arisen originally from the social structure of the Ottoman empire, which dominated Bulgaria for over 500 years. The Turks oppressed all conquered people equally. Only Turks were allowed to amass wealth, which meant that class divisions did not develop among Bulgarians.

The country's isolation from European democratic trends also made it easy for the Communist Party to unite its interests with those of the people. Bulgaria has always remained close to its big Slav brother in Russia who liberated it from the Ottoman empire as well as from the Nazis. This friendship almost became unity when Zhivkov proposed to Nikita Khrushchev that Bulgaria should become the sixteenth Republic of the Soviet Union. The offer was rejected, but he continued to receive strong Soviet support.

Despite this, the country's economic growth rates began to slow in 1977, and the decline accelerated in 1984. The foreign debt was then $3.6 billion, but by 1989 it had rocketed to $10.5 billion. The cost of servicing this debt is $1 billion a year, which is 40 percent more than the total annual value of Bulgaria's exports to the West. The slide into financial crisis was camouflaged in the early 1980s by the technique of selling imported Soviet oil abroad for hard currency. This angered the Soviet leadership, who were making a sacrifice by selling the oil cheaply to help an ally.

To make matters worse, investment had been directed into the wrong sectors. Heavy, inefficient and outdated industry and grandiose construction schemes soaked up funds while agriculture, tourism and light engineering barely staggered along. Most of the population have jobs, but few do very much work. Salaries are fixed and there is little incentive, with the old Communist bloc adage prevailing: they pretend to pay us and we pretend to work. As a result most people seek paid work in their spare time.

By the late 1980s, Bulgarian society and its Communist Party were in a deep crisis that mirrored that of the Soviet Union. The country's industry was clinically dead, despite constant attempts over a 20-year period to make it more efficient and to introduce modern scientific and technological methods. All the reforms failed and Zhivkov's plans that were regularly presented to the Central Committee collapsed into managerial reshuffles and the usual exhortations for greater effort. On each occasion, there followed a return to the certainties of the centralised command and administer system.

A similar fate befell agriculture. The older generation who remained on the land no longer owned it and were alienated from their work. A haphazard and unpopular collectivisation led many people to concentrate on their gardens and allotments, which ensured food supplies for them, and for family members who had migrated to the towns and cities. The capital Sofia now has one million residents, three times the population of 20 years ago.

The country has also suffered an ecological disaster. The cities are choked with air pollution, way above international standards – up to 17 times higher for some pollutants – and the Black Sea is dead below 200 metres. The Trakia Plain, which was once the most fertile agricultural land, is now poisoned with heavy metals from a nearby ferrous metals plant. And after the Chernobyl nuclear disaster, Bulgarians were not warned of the dangers, which has resulted in the country suffering the highest level of health damage outside the Soviet Union.

Bulgarians have never faced such acute shortages as their Soviet comrades, although their women still spend endless hours in queues, mainly as a result of indifferent service and a highly inefficient distribution system. More recently, things have got much worse, with many staples such as cheese, eggs, coffee and most vegetables more difficult to find. Things got worse still after the exodus of one-third of the ethnic Turks in the summer of 1989. Most of the hard working Turks were country people and much of the autumn harvest was lost. The problem will increase in the future as even less was done to prepare for future harvests. In February 1990, powdered baby milk became unavailable, except in the hard currency shops that serve only foreigners. As a result, the environmental group Ecoglasnost launched a national campaign which included an appeal to the United Nations for humanitarian aid.

Finding consumer goods, or getting them repaired, has been a nightmare for Bulgarians for decades. A new Russian Lada car means a wait of between 15 and 20 years, although the East German Trabant can be obtained in less than one year. There have been no vacuum cleaners for 10 years, and although the country produces food mixers and refrigerators, they are mostly exported.

Suppliers in warehouses and shops are therefore in a strong position, leading to widespread pilfering, embezzlement and bribery. Bulgarians desperately need 'connections' (known locally as *vruski*) to make up for the deficiencies. These include teachers, who will give higher marks to ensure a place in further education, or a degree; doctors and surgeons who allow queue jumping; and anyone in the *nomenklatura* who can smooth the bureaucratic path.

Since every aspect of Bulgarian life was dominated by the Communist Party, the crisis has naturally been reflected throughout its structures. It became riddled with careerism, nepotism and corruption, and is ideologically bankrupt. The Party lost credibility by failing to deliver on its promise to increase living standards, and its increasing remoteness. Most top leaders were middle-aged male executives, with women and members of minority groups given few opportunities. They were fighting to preserve their privileges – although one lecturer at the Higher Party School accurately pointed out that even being a top official in Bulgaria hardly provided a better lifestyle than that of the average farmer in Iowa.

Political idealism was squeezed out of the organisation, and most of the pre-war Communists, the revered 'fighters against fascism and capitalism' who had established the system, had long since vacated the scene. Young people were rejecting the Party, which still claimed to take care of all their needs, but in fact only regimented their lives. Official publications, which had in the past denounced long hair, tight trousers, short skirts and rock music, began to sound off against a new 'negative phenomenon': football hooliganism. The Komsomol (Young Communist League) started attacking the country's youth, who they said were too interested in drugs, pop music and Western fashion. Then, as if to prove how remote they were from their contemporaries, they began a campaign of interrupting discos to deliver political education lectures.

Into this political vacuum the old Balkan nationalist flag was raised. Zhivkov had declared his intention of creating a unified socialist state, and was reversing his earlier policies of giving some degree of autonomy to ethnic minorities. Children at school were taught knowledge of the fatherland, and in 1981 the 1300th anniversary of the first Bulgarian state was lavishly celebrated. The Turkish minority, one million strong, lost their schools, university faculty and newspapers.

By 1985, the Turks were being forced against their will to change their names. According to Amnesty International, 100 were killed and many thousands imprisoned during the campaign. It became a crime to speak Turkish, Islamic rites such as circumcision, burial customs, and traditional dress were banned, and many mosques closed. Some 200,000 ethnic Bulgarians who practise the Muslim religion (Pomaks) had been forcibly renamed 13 years earlier. Although several people were killed during this operation, it passed by almost unnoticed.

Zhivkov and his closest advisers were worried that while the Turkish population was increasing, the Bulgarians barely had sufficient children to maintain numbers. He feared the growth of revanchism in Turkey, and pointed to the Turkish invasion of Cyprus to prove his case. These fears provided a useful diversion from troubles closer to home, but the Turkish Prime Minister Turgut Ozal, who was also facing internal problems, welcomed a foreign diversion. In order to direct attention away from his own bad record against the Kurdish minorities, Ozal began to denounce Bulgaria's abuse against its Turkish minority.

In May 1989, Turks in north-east and south-east Bulgaria held a series of demonstrations to coincide with the Paris human rights' meeting of the Conference on Security and Cooperation in Europe (CSCE). These demonstrations and the violent official reaction to them triggered a series of events that eventually led to the ousting of Zhivkov and the ending of his authoritarian system.

The process began when a group of Turkish activists joined a hunger strike in early May. They aimed to attract world attention to the plight of the ethnic Turks who live in close knit communities where a sense of collective victimisation is nurtured. Heads of the large extended Turkish families and community leaders wield great influence, which ensured big turnouts for demonstrations organised in Kaolinovo, Todor Ikonomovo and in the Tolbukhin and Varna areas.

The demonstrations were organised by two groups: the Committee to Support Vienna '89; and the Democratic League for Human Rights, which was founded by Turks who had spent years in the Banubean prison island of Belen for refusing to adopt Bulgarian names. Both organisations were closely associated with the Independent Society for Human Rights. The demonstrators had three demands: the right to speak Turkish; the right freely to practice the Muslim religion; and the restoration of their original names.

Up to 15,000 people turned out, to be met by the full force of the state. They were surrounded by troops and militia who used dogs, clubs, smoke bombs, tanks, helicopters and guns against unarmed people. According to official figures, seven people were killed and 40 injured, but local people put the figure at 60 deaths, 100 injured, and thousands arrested. Those jailed were released after a few days but over 5000 were deported to Turkey in late May and early June. These included the organisers of the demonstrations and many community leaders.

The towns and villages where demonstrations took place were sealed off by military road blocks and communications were cut. Curfews of up to four days were imposed and soldiers patrolled the streets, beating and arresting people indiscriminately and seeking out those who joined the demonstrations for special treatment. Zhivkov and his closest adviser, Milko Balev, knew of no other way to deal with such insubordination. Their finely tuned system of repression was well geared for dealing with the Turkish minority. Interior Minister Georgi Tanev had been Communist Party Secretary in the predominantly Turkish area of Kurdjali, where he distinguished himself in 1984 and 1985 by using the most brutal means of ensuring a speedy adoption of Bulgarian names. Tanev replaced Dimitar Stoyanov, who had been promoted to full Politburo status after 14 years as head of internal security, a position from which he had overseen the whole assimilation campaign and became a close Zhivkov trusty.

Evidence of atrocities committed against the May demonstrations was presented by eyewitnesses, participants and organisers to the Paris human rights' conference. Bulgaria was duly condemned for violating the fundamental right to free expression, assembly and organisation. In the reaction that followed, the European Community cancelled negotiations for a new trade treaty. It was this, and the international opprobrium suffered by Bulgaria that created a determination among those closest to the world's hostility to act against Zhivkov.

These included Foreign Minister Petar Mladenov, Defence Minister Dobri Dzhurov and Foreign Economic Relations Minister Andrey Loukanov. They were already part of a sullen but silent opposition that was becoming increasingly worried about the growing personal power of Zhivkov. The 1984–85 campaign to change Turkish names, for example, was decided by him without any official consultation or sanction. But, at the end of May 1989, Zhivkov's position remained unassailable and on the rare occasions that he referred decisions to the ruling Politburo he was assured of unanimity.

No criticism was uttered when arrests began on 26 May of six human rights' activists who were alleged to have incited the Turks to join hunger strikes. They were Dr Konstantin Trenchev, Nikolai Kolev and Todor Gagalov of Podkrepa, Anton Zaprianov and Hassan Beyalov of the Independent Society for Human Rights and Father Hristofer Subev of the Religious Rights' Committee. All six went on hunger strike, were force fed, and subsequently became a *cause célèbre*. Defence committees were organised on their behalf, petitions circulated and regular news provided on the Bulgarian services of Radio Free Europe, Deutsche Welle and the BBC. These foreign based radio stations played an important role as independent sources of information, against the tightly controlled state media.

On the eve of the Paris conference Zhivkov addressed the nation and accused the Turkish Government of provoking the disturbances in Bulgaria for their own expansionist ends. He continued to promote the fiction that Bulgaria contained no ethnic Turks, but merely a Muslim minority whose ancestors had been forced to adopt the Islamic religion during the Ottoman empire. Zhivkov then announced that Bulgaria would issue foreign travel passports to all citizens who wanted them on 1 September, and was therefore adhering to the Helsinki and Vienna accords. He called on Turkey to open its borders and to accept every 'Bulgarian Muslim' who wanted to go there. This declaration was greeted by 'spontaneous' anti-Turkish demonstrations around the country, organised by the Communist controlled Fatherland Front. In the following 10 weeks, 350,000 people fled before Turkey effectively closed the border on 22 August. It was the biggest population movement in Europe since World War II. The flow was then controlled to about 2000 per week and some 80,000 returned.

In an attempt to stem the flow of emigrants, and save the crucial tobacco crop in the south-west Gotse Delchev area, local officials refused to issue passports. In six key villages, strikes and demonstrations began on 15 August which were met by an invasion by internal security forces who sealed off the area and forced the people back to work. The military occupation remained effective until mid-December.

The disruption to Bulgaria's political, social and economic life was immense. Whole villages emptied, factories ground to a halt, and crop and farm animals were left untended. Those who had decided to go also stopped working, and this made the crisis worse. Zhivkov responded with appeals to patriotism, and by issuing new decrees that lengthened the working week and introduced the direction of labour. These actions helped to fuel resentment against the Turkish minority, who were accused of carelessly abandoning their homeland.

At the same time there was some sympathy for the Turks among Bulgarians. Television nightly showed thousands of families who had waited for days at the border with their belongings. This brought home the human drama that was being played out to serve an amorphous national interest.

Zhivkov had clearly gone too far. His actions had scared some of his closest Politburo allies and encouraged his silent opposition to act. Bulgaria's dissident movement began to take more risks, and speak out more boldly as they guessed a leadership crisis was looming. International opinion was unremittingly hostile, and Zhivkov's isolation was confirmed when Gorbachov refused to back his anti-Turkish policy when they met in June. Gorbachov had been seeking closer relations with Turkey and was furious that his efforts had been thwarted by a close Warsaw Pact ally.

The opposition movement survived and grew, despite deportations, detention, travel restrictions, internal exile, constant surveillance and the frequent use of force and weapons by the authorities. As fast as the Government deported leaders of groups like the Independent Society for Human Rights, new people emerged to take their places. The society contained many former political prisoners who had become toughened by pressure. They were particularly hated by the authorities because they refused to compromise on the rights of the ethnic Turks. The society's leader, research chemist Roumen Vodenicharov, removed from the organisation's leadership any who opposed Muslim rights. But the society never developed a wide base of support.

Another Independent Society stalwart, former sea captain Lyubomir Sobadjiev, sought broader objectives and launched a group called Citizens' Initiative. His aim was to coordinate dissident activity and to provide a stimulus for direct political challenges to the Communist Party. Sobadjiev was put under enormous pressure by the authorities and his organisation was launched too late to play a major part before the downfall of Zhivkov.

The high powered Independent Discussion Club for the Support of Perestroika and Glasnost contained many well known cultural and academic figures such as Professors Zhelyu Zhelev, Patko Simeonov and Chavdar Kyurianovi; the poet Blaga Dimitrova and the journalist Koprinka Chervenkova. Half of the club's 250 members were in the Communist Party, although some were expelled and lost their jobs. The club spoke out in support of the Turkish minority and presented a petition to the National Assembly. This was a direct challenge to Zhivkov and was met with total silence, which indicated that a split existed in the Politburo.

The top leadership was also divided about how to react to the dissident environmental group Ecoglasnost, led by Bulgaria's most popular actor, Petar Slabakov. The environmentalists were demanding the right to participate as a non-government organisation in a CSCE follow-up conference on the environment due to be held in Sofia between 16 October and 3 November. They approached Western embassies for support, and produced some highly impressive research papers. The group proposed that their secretary, Dr Petar Beron, Bulgaria's leading zoologist, should be the conference's Executive Secretary. This proposition was ignored, although Beron was surprisingly included as an adviser to Bulgaria's official delegation. Both the club and Ecoglasnost had deliberately chosen less confrontational objectives, with the aim of providing a cover for opposition activity. But, until the CSCE environment conference provided an opportunity, they had failed to achieve a public face.

Before the arrival of the delegates, diplomats and journalists, the Bulgarian authorities attempted to regain ground by releasing on bail on 4 September the six human rights' activists imprisoned three months earlier. An unprecedented public campaign had been waged for their freedom with the Minister of Justice, Svetla Dashkolov, and the official Human Rights' Committee also privately applying pressure in their favour. The six were held illegally, they had waited weeks longer than the law allowed for indictments to be issued, and the authorities knew that they were on weak ground and would have problems making the charges stick. The opposition was encouraged by this development and estimated that if they made a major impact during the conference, and established contacts with international organisations, they might avoid a heavy crackdown when the conference ended.

In the event the opposition mounted an historic challenge, and organised the first unofficial meetings, demonstrations and press conferences for 40 years that were not immediately broken up by the militia. At the conference the Bulgarian Government had been thrown on to the defensive by Western delegates, notably the British and US, who strongly attacked the country's appalling human rights' record. For 12 days, Ecoglasnost appeared in a popular spot in central Sofia with placards and collected signatures on petitions demanding public consultation on a river diversion scheme. They launched their 'Ecocharter 89' at a packed press conference and held a meeting that filled a cinema auditorium, leaving people standing on the stairs, in the foyer and hundreds more outside.

During the same period, the Independent Society for Human Rights began a series of open air meetings at Sofia's Southern Park, and the Committee for Religious Rights held services in the Santa Dimitar Church to pray for the success of the opposition movement. Dr Konstantin Trenchev, out on bail, launched Podkrepa's programme, linking it with Poland's Solidarity and other international organisations. A majority on the Communist Party's Politburo was horrified at such open opposition, and instigated immediate action.

On 26 October, after failing to convince Ecoglasnost's supporters to move out of central Sofia to a remote suburb, the uniformed militia and security police, the Derzhavna Sigurnost (DS), lost patience. They savagely beat up and arrested 40 Ecoglasnost demonstrators in full view of American and French diplomats, conference delegates and journalists. One British journalist was also attacked by a DS officer who smashed his camera to prevent him recording the scene. The DS then rounded up and assaulted a number of opposition leaders and deported them from Sofia to the provinces. Some were accused of petty crimes and one, Lyubomir Sobadjiev, of espionage. The reaction at the CSCE conference was inevitable. Western and non-aligned delegates invoked protest procedures and threatened to walk out unless a satisfactory explanation was given.

An unprecedented apology was delivered by Bulgaria's Environment Minister Nikolai Dyulgerov, who admitted that the militia and DS had 'overstepped the mark'; the dissidents were then allowed to return to Sofia. Zhivkov moved quickly to try to bolster his rapidly eroding authority, issuing a 14,000 word statement about the progress of *perestroika* in Bulgaria. It was full of his usual liberal sounding phrases and aimed to persuade hardliners that the party was still in control. He hoped that with a few concessions to public opinion, the opposition and foreign diplomats, his credibility would be restored.

Unimpressed, the opposition continued its public campaign, culminating on 3 November in a demonstration of 5000 Ecoglasnost supporters in Alexander Nevsky Cathedral Square in Sofia. They marched to the National Assembly and delivered a petition containing 11,500 signatures. On 24 October, Petar Mladenov, who had served as Todor Zhivkov's Foreign Minister for over 18 years, sensed that the time was right and delivered a letter of resignation. That set in train a behind-the-scenes leadership crisis which culminated in the removal of Zhivkov from power 16 days later.

Mladenov's resignation letter accused Zhivkov of establishing a regime of personal power and of 'eating out of the same trough as the rotten dictator Ceausescu'. He said that no minister was able to

A young pro-democracy demonstrator in Sofia makes her point by redesigning a portrait of Todor Zhivkov. (Photo: Rajtik-Zoja/Gamma)

function properly, as all decisions were subject to the whims of Zhivkov and his number two, Milko Balev. Mladenov accused Zhivkov of promoting his half-witted and alcoholic 37-year-old son Vladimir to the job of Central Committee Secretary of Culture, and of using 'rough methods' to get his own way. Mladenov concluded by appealing to his Central Committee comrades to protect him and his family's lives from Zhivkov's revenge.

The resignation was rejected, although Mladenov failed to attend a meeting with his Turkish counterpart, Yilmaz Merut, on 30 October. Zhivkov reasserted his authority by announcing a Central Committee meeting for 10 November, where personnel and other changes would be made. Mladenov then resumed his duties and a few days before the meeting he visited Peking. During this trip, he made a crucial stopover in Moscow, where Mikhail Gorbachov confirmed his backing for the ousting of Zhivkov.

Mladenov had secured a shaky six to four majority on the Politburo. He first won the backing of Defence Minister Dobri Dzhurov and the Prime Minister Georgi Atanasov, and then approached three Zhivkov loyalists who knew that events were running against them. They wanted a peaceful transfer of power, and could themselves be let down lightly. These were two of Zhivkov's wartime comrades, ideology chief Yordan Yotov, and Fatherland Front leader Pencho Kubadinski; and Sofia Party Secretary Ivan Panev. Mladenov promised they would not be thrown out of the Politburo immediately and that any changes would not be too radical. The other three members were too closely associated with Zhivkov to be dislodged: Milko Balev and Dimitar Stoyanov had blood on their hands after the anti-Turkish campaign, and Grisha Filipov was completely in the Zhivkov mould.

Hours before the crucial Central Committee meeting a group that included Dzhurov and Yotov approached Zhivkov and told him that he had to step down as Party General Secretary. They told him that he would receive the usual accolades on his resignation and that he could stay on as State President. Zhivkov accepted, because although he had the support of security chief Dimitar Stoyanov, he was uncertain that he could rely on the backing of all the security forces. In any event, it had been made clear that the Army under Dzhurov wanted him out.

In fact, the promise was broken. After Zhivkov had read his General Secretary's report to the Central Committee, Georgi Atanasov announced that Zhivkov was resigning from all his posts. The event was shown live on television and Zhivkov was visibly shaken by the announcement. His jaw dropped and his head slumped. He left the meeting and was effectively placed under house arrest.

News of Zhivkov's fall took most people by surprise. The only hints of it had come from the Soviet Embassy in London, the Soviet Consulate in Bulgaria's second city Plovdiv, and from Soviet Foreign

Ministry spokesman Gennadi Gerasimov in Moscow. This indicates just how closely involved Mikhail Gorbachov was in assisting Mladenov to take power. The two have known each other since they were students together in Moscow in the early 1960s. Bulgarians reacted ecstatically to Zhivkov's removal and there were nationwide celebrations. Over 50,000 people attended a pro-democracy rally, but the meeting had a holiday atmosphere and was more inclined to welcome Mladenov than make heavy demands on him.

Before the opposition rally, Mladenov had already met leading dissidents, removed the key hardliners from the party leadership, and reinstated to their jobs and Party membership all those thrown out for the dissident activities. He also held a National Assembly meeting where an amnesty for political prisoners was announced; made sweeping Government changes; eliminated anti-dissent sections of the penal code; and declared his support for free elections. The official Fatherland Front also held a 15,000-strong, pro-Mladenov rally the day before the opposition gathered. By these moves, Mladenov vaulted ahead of the opposition and also managed to placate the conservative forces inside the Communist Party.

All the problems that beset Bulgaria were blamed by Mladenov and his new number two, Andrey Loukanov, on the old authoritarian system and on Zhivkov personally. They undertook to reshape the Party's personnel and policies and direct the Party towards becoming a European-style democratic socialist party. They also prepared to move towards free multi-party elections, ending the Communist monopoly on power, and restoring the rights of the Muslim and Turkish minorities.

These actions pre-empted most of the opposition's demands. Two weeks after Mladenov's coup, the president of the Club for Perestroika and Glasnost, Petko Simeonov admitted: 'Our opposition is weak, we are not well organised, and we have no clear ideology or leaders. We could bring out a million people, but at the moment we have nothing to tell them.' By early December the main opposition groups had joined together in a Union of Democratic Forces (UDF), and the formerly subservient Agrarian Party, which had 'shared power' with the Communists since 1948, declared its independence. Other parties such as the Social Democratic Party and the Agrarian Party of Nikola Petkov, which had been banned for over 40 years, were re-formed. New parties like the Greens emerged and Ecoglasnost, Podkrepa and the Independent Society for Human Rights gained new supporters. In addition new political groups have sprung up around the country and new youth and student groups have formed.

The UDF has since attempted to set the political agenda and to force the Communist Party to relinquish its totalitarian power more quickly. They joined round table talks with the Communists in January 1990 but discussions soon became bogged down. The talks stopped as the opposition demanded a headquarters, a daily newspaper, and full media coverage of the round table. Subsequently talks turned to reducing the power of the Ministry of the Interior and removing Communist Party organisation in the workplaces.

The UDF has been reluctant to incorporate newly formed groups or the trade unions, Komsomol or women's groups, once Communist-controlled but now, they claim, independent of the Party. Suspicion and the fear of inviting a Trojan horse into its ranks has weakened opposition unity. It also lost some credibility by rejecting an invitation to join a coalition government. The ironical result of this was that on 8 February, under new Prime Minister Andrey Loukanov, Bulgaria swore in its first entirely Communist government.

For the opposition to make headway in the multi-party elections it will be vital for the UDF to present a joint slate of candidates. The electoral system being proposed for Bulgaria is the alternative list system, which gives more weight to parties than to individual candidates. This will favour the Communist Party, whose standing in an opinion poll in late January remained over 30 percent. But the UDF scored 13 percent, and two of its affiliates a further five percent each, even before their leaders were well known or their newspapers had appeared. The same poll revealed that the most popular personalities were Defence Minister Dobri Dzhurov, with Mladenov and Louka-nov close behind. The Army was the most popular institution, reflecting a widespread belief that it was the Army that ensured Bulgaria's bloodless escape from totalitarianism.

The Communist Party continued its political house-cleaning by reversing Zhivkov's anti-Turkish policies and by restoring minority rights. It also quickly and effectively defused an ugly nationalist backlash whipped up by conservative elements inside the Party. These events were followed by an extraordinary congress in early February which adopted a new European-style democratic socialist manifesto and revised the Party's organisational structures. More than 50 percent of the regional secretaries were replaced; 85 percent of delegates were first timers, although the average age remained high; and less than 20 percent of the previous national leadership was re-elected. Despite this, the congress was criticised for being old fashioned and for its poor standards of debate.

The opposition is still facing a formidable enemy. The new Communist Party leaders have already opened negotiations to seek economic and financial aid for the country, and are presenting themselves as the only national leadership able to resolve the crisis.

They have acknowledged the Party's role in causing Bulgaria's problems, but have had some success in distancing themselves from Zhivkovism.

Andrey Loukanov has been hailed in some quarters as Bulgaria's Gorbachov, but he also impressed diplomats as having many of the features of a Western conservative politician. A combination of these objective features, plus the powerful factor of inertia, could give Bulgaria's Communist Party victory in the first free election, in spite of 45 years of mismanagement, authoritarianism and corruption.

CZECHOSLOVAKIA
The velvet revolution

Spring 1968	Reforms begin under Government headed by Alexander Dubcek.
20–21 August 1968	Warsaw Pact forces invade Czechoslovakia: Dubcek deposed.
17 November 1989	Peaceful march by 50,000 people in Prague violently suppressed by police.
18 November 1989	People gather in Wenceslas Square to protest at the police violence.
19 November 1989	Civic Forum formed by Vaclav Havel and friends.
20 November 1989	200,000 demonstrate in Prague for freedom and democracy.
23 November 1989	Workers pledge support for general strike: Dubcek speaks in Bratislava.
24 November 1989	Milos Jakes and entire Politburo resign.
27 November 1989	General strike.
3 December 1989	New Government formed with Communists still dominating.
4 December 1989	300,000 protest make-up of the new Government.
7 December 1989	Government collapses.
10 December 1989	New Government with majority of non-Communists sworn into office.
30 December 1989	Vaclav Havel elected President.

A stuffed Alsation guard dog, its yellow teeth bared in an eternal snarl, stands on a plinth in the National Security Museum hidden away on Ke Karlovu Street in Prague. There are many other curious items to be seen in this museum, which no one has got round to closing: an entire wall prickling with revolvers – seized from 'spies' in the early 1950s; another wall arrayed with rifles, thrusting out at a martial angle to challenge the visitor; a room full of electronic listening devices and other 'national security' nick-nacks. But the dog with the eternal snarl is, perhaps, the most bizarre exhibit in this bizarre museum, dedicated to the armoury of Stalinism. A note on the plinth explains the dog's presence: 'Despite modern technology used in our border, the dog remains a very important friend of the border guards'. You can even buy a postcard of the snarl, should you wish.

A visit to the museum, a 10-minute walk from the city centre over the viaduct from the Gottwaldova subway stop, is a necessary reminder of the brute power that kept the Communist Party in place after it overthrew democracy in 1948. The dogs, the guns and the listening devices were used again in 1968 to back up the Soviet tanks which rolled in to crush the liberal Prague Spring, brought about by the reformist government of Alexander Dubcek. For the four decades the Communist Party enjoyed power, it relied not on popular support but on these sinister exhibits which have, almost in the blinking of an eye, become tourist curiosities.

The revolution in Czechoslovakia only took ten days. As well as being the fastest, it was also the tidiest, the most peaceful, the wittiest and the only one with dialogue written by a playwright, Vaclav Havel. The backcloth was Prague city centre, so beautiful you could almost eat it, a baroque chocolate box of a place. You could call it the designer revolution, but such sardonic judgements devalue the difficulty of opposing a regime which used every secret policeman's trick to maintain its privileges. The Czechs and the Slovaks had to be brave to win their freedom. (The country is made up of two halves, the Czech and Slovak republics. Prague is both the Czech and the national capital; Bratislava the Slovakian capital.)

No one lost their life in the Czechoslovakian revolution – although a 'death' which never took place was the catalyst. But blood was spilled; it could well have been a lot bloodier and more violent. The other side had all the weapons of brute power to hand. Velvet smooth as it eventually turned out to be, the Czechoslovakian revolution was never as easy as it looked.

Friday 17 November – Bloody Friday – was the start. History provided official sanction for a students' march which turned sour for the regime. In 1939 a Czech student, Jan Opletal, was killed by Nazi troops during demonstrations against Hitler's move into Czechoslovakia. The official Socialist Youth Movement, the SSM, gave its backing to a march commemorating, not Opletal's death, but the anniversary of his funeral. The march started with a crowd of about 20,000 gathering at the medical university. From the beginning, it was clear that present repression – rather than that of the Nazis half a century ago – was the target of the protesters. Many carried banners calling for 'Freedom', 'Justice for all' and 'Release political prisoners': innocuous enough, one would have thought. But a few years earlier Amnesty International reported that a 23-year-old graffiti artist who had scribbled on a wall 'The end of socialism! What do you think of that, Vladimir?' got 20 months in prison for his undignified reference to Lenin.

As the marchers moved off, the regime expressed its displeasure. The Czechoslovak Communist Party's ideology chief, Jan Fotjik, told reporters while on a visit to Moscow: 'I'm certain we can establish a dialogue with reasonable people, but there can be no dialogue with those who set out to destroy our society'. Tough words, but the marchers may also have suspected that Mikhail Gorbachov had taken the chance to tell Fotjik that the Soviet Union had no intention of sending in the tanks in 1989 as his predecessor Brezhnev had done in 1968. Officially, Fotjik was told in Moscow that the Czechoslovak leadership should embark on a 'thorough analysis of the past', thinly disguised Kremlin-speak for a ticking-off. In Czechoslovakia, when comment was unfree, jokes were sacred. The following political joke encapsulated the realities: to save Communism, they said, Czech tanks would have to roll into Moscow.

The march, growing all the while, threaded its way to the national cemetery at Vysehrad, the burial place of the composers Smetana and Dvorak. By this stage, the numbers had grown to about 50,000, the biggest-ever popular demonstration since the heady days of the Prague Spring. The crowd's chants grew more vociferous, calling not just for freedom, but for the dismissal of the Communist Party First Secretary, effectively the country's ruler, Milos Jakes. The banners seemed to become more robust: 'We don't want the Communist Party', 'Forty years are enough' and 'Jakes – this is your end'. One of the largest banners of all carried President Gorbachov's appeal for *perestroika*: 'If not now, when?'

At the cemetery, according to the agreement with the police, the march should have ended. The majority of marchers, especially the older ones, started to go home. But a core of students shouted 'To Wenceslas Square', and turned back for the centre of the town. As the students, now numbering about 3000, walked up Narodni Street on the way to the square, they came upon a wall of riot police, white-helmeted, carrying plastic shields and heavy truncheons. In the

A girl lights a candle on a makeshift shrine in Narodni Street in Prague. (Photo: Roger Hutchings)

preceding weeks as tension had built up, the riot police had practised their tactics again and again. The moment of confrontation had arrived.

Pavlina Rousova and Otto Urban, both students at Prague's Charles University, take up the story: 'We sat down and sang hymns, the national anthem, even old Beatles hits. We chanted: "We have no weapons". The only things we had with us were candles and some flowers, which we gave to the police. They used loud-hailers to shout "Go home", but they had blocked our path.'

Another squad of riot police had come up behind the students. They were trapped. The stand-off lasted a couple of hours. At around 9.10 pm, a police car drove into the crowd, causing panic. Riot police lunged at students, clubbing them as they scattered. Wax from the candles spilled on to the road, so police and students fell tumbling to the ground on the slippery, treacherous surface. Blood, too, spattered the ground. A woman bystander said: 'The police took the people in the first row of the demonstration and they beat them mercilessly. They would not let the young people go. They brought in buses and arrested them all.' An art academy student, Martin Polach, said afterwards about the police brutality: 'You could literally hear the bones cracking'.

Vaclav, a reporter from *Mlady Svet* (*Young World*), was carried in the crush across the street towards a passageway where people appeared to be getting away. As he got closer he saw that the police had formed a corridor, beating heavily any student who attempted to run the gauntlet. He saw three 'red berets' – special troops – attacking a young woman. One of them snatched her hair, and banged her head against a wall. When she fell, they kicked her. She lay silent; the three started to laugh.

Edward Lucas, a reporter from *The Independent* newspaper who had been watching the riot police laying into the students, was himself led away by two uniformed policemen; as they did so, a plainclothes man knocked him, unconscious, to the ground. An ITN cameraman, Philip Bye, was also beaten up. Both incidents prompted protests from the British Foreign Office minister William Waldegrave and the British ambassador in Prague, Lawrence O'Keefe.

Pavlina and Otto managed to run into a side alley, Mikulandska Street, and found themselves in a courtyard. As their friends were beaten up, they and about 50 others found sanctuary in a friend's flat. They turned off the lights and stood in the dark like statues, hardly daring to breathe, listening to the turmoil outside on the street: dogs barking, shouts of 'Hands up, you whore', thumps, stamping feet, screams that seemed that much more piercing in the silence of the flat. They tried to hide the revolutionary leaflets they had with them, pushing them under the sofa. They waited for the beatings to stop, fearful that the police would discover their hiding place. For Pavlina, it was the worst moment: 'This was really terrible'. She shuddered at the re-telling, and not simply from the below-zero cold of a Prague winter. When they finally slipped home in ones and twos, much later, the freedom marchers were demoralised and afraid.

The following day the Communist Party mouthpiece, *Rude Pravo*, published the blandest of accounts: 'Police were called in to preserve public order in the city centre. They checked the identity of the demonstrators, and approximately 100 people were detained at the police station. By 10 pm peace was restored to the city centre.'

It was a classic lie by omission. The danger for the Communist Party was that Prague's rumour machine – which faced no reliable, honest competition from the Government-controlled press – worked overtime. The whole city knew that the police had behaved with unconscionable violence; worse, stories that a young mathematics student, Martin Smid, had been killed by the police began to spread. The story came from Smid's girlfriend, Drahomira Drascka, who told Petr Uhl, a fearless human rights' and Charter 77 activist. Uhl was a well known critic, lambasting the Government from a left wing, Trotskyite perspective. Drahomira, who said she was also beaten, told Charter 77 that police informed her at the scene that Smid had been 'finished off' in a darkened side street.

The rumours about Smid's death were picked up and amplified on Saturday evening by Voice of America and Radio Free Europe. The broadcasts gave new force to the opposition, which became bolder in its demands. There had been sporadic outbreaks of unrest in Prague before, on the anniversary of the invasion in August the previous year and, at the start of 1989, on the twenty-first anniversary of the suicide of Jan Palach, who set fire to himself in Wenceslas Square on 16 January. But, this time, the atmosphere was different. The city was crackling with tension.

The pressure was probably greatest in a gloomy concrete and glass office block, painted a sickly kind of beige, in Bartolomejska Street. The tedious slogan in giant red capitals which was hung over its front – 'Eternal solidarity with the Soviet Union' – gave no clue that this was the headquarters of the secret police, the Statni Bezpecnost or STB. After the riot police had overdone the blood-letting, it was up to the STB to arrange the cover-up. They succeeded in producing not one, but two students called Martin Smid. The Government claimed that one Smid had taken no part in Friday's march and that the other had demonstrated but had suffered no injuries. They broadcast this statement over the loudspeakers at Wenceslas Square, using the special wheedling tone of police states on the slide. Their story was, in fact, true, but nobody believed them. Czechs, connoisseurs of deception, thought the Government was lying yet again and rebelled because of a non-existent martyr, an exquisite irony for a nation that has had its share of real ones.

The authorities acted with predictable stupidity, arresting all those close to the case: Petr Uhl and Drahomira, as well as two others, Tomas Hradilek, a spokesman for Charter 77, and Jan Shudomel, a Pacifist Movement leader. The public testimony of Uhl and Drahomira, once they had realised their mistake, would have done much to take the heat out of the rumours; but the regime of Milos Jakes was too dull witted to realise that.

That weekend, as the STB traced a multitude of Smids, the people grew outraged. An archway in Narodni Street where some of the beatings took place quickly became a place of pilgrimage. Someone daubed a cross on a wall nearby, two strokes in black spraypaint. Hundreds of candles were lit at the makeshift shrine. To the astonishment of the crowd, two Soviet soldiers went up to the spot and added their own candles. Wreaths were laid on the darkening but still visible bloodstains; people milling in the streets wore black armbands or ribbons in mourning.

Although Smid's death was genuinely deniable, the level of police violence on 'Bloody Friday' was not. Dr Jan Pelant, aged 39, a witty mathematician with a physical likeness to the middle-aged Lenin, had taken part in the demonstration, but had peeled off with the majority of people after it had reached Vysehrad Cemetery. Never an active dissident, Dr Pelant's dislike of the regime was expressed by private contempt and his refusal to join the Communist Party. When he had been a student in 1969 and had protested about the Soviet invasion, he had been taken for a ride on the 'prison lift', which meant running a gauntlet of secret police, who beat him with rubber truncheons. He had no faith in the Government's denials. 'When I heard how brutally the police had beaten the students, I decided that enough was enough. The next day I went to Wenceslas Square and waited for the police to arrest me. But they didn't come.' His personal decision to resist the regime, after 20 years of mute, glum acquiescence was repeated across the city, one by one by one. The numbers added up.

But so far only students and intellectuals like Dr Pelant were daring to stand out in freezing temperatures. The pioneer revolutionaries all got bad colds. They called it 'liberation influenza'.

That Saturday afternoon, the actors joined them. After a heated discussion at the Realistic Theatre in Prague, the actors not only demanded an independent inquiry into the police violence but proposed a general strike on Monday 27 November if their demands were not met. They had a week and a day to enlist mass popular support.

On Sunday night up to 20,000 people took over Wenceslas Square, and then marched around Prague, bearing the national flag and shouting out some of Friday's chants, such as 'Freedom', and some new ones too. The spiciest was 'Jakes to the shovel', a Czech version of 'On yer bike', but with an added stab: when many intellectuals and talented people lost their jobs after the Prague Spring, quite a few found themselves working as stokers. The riot police, barring the crowd's route to Hradcany Castle, the seat of power, were greeted with cries of 'Murderers' and 'Gestapo'. The crowd halted in front of the National Theatre to applaud its actors, on strike in support of the students. A matinee performance of Smetana's Bartered Bride in the National Theatre was shelved; the opera-goers were instead treated to a revolutionary declaration by the 150 members of the production, read out by the director, Ladislav Stros.

The regime was beginning to lose its nerve, but things were still very much in the balance. All the weapons of brute power were still in place; the workers in this workers' state had so far stayed at home. As events hotted up, the pressure on Milos Jakes and the man who opposed him, Vaclav Havel, grew to breaking point.

The verdict of history on Jakes will not be a particularly polite one. He was the heir to a dishonourable, even murderous, succession of grey stooges who used brute power to rule Czechoslovakia, first under the Nazis, then under the Communists. In December 1987, Jakes took over as First Secretary of the Communist Party from Gustav Husak, who was elevated to the presidency. Husak, a Slovak, was the Quisling the Soviets used to justify their invasion. Far from being a new man, Jakes had been, as chairman of the Party's Control Commission from 1968 to 1977, Husak's witchfinder-general, personally extinguishing the careers of 600,000 of the Party's 1.5 million members in the mass purge which followed the invasion.

One political joke doing the rounds before the revolution was that Jakes would fail a lie-detector test by uttering the phrase 'I think'. Another: 'What's the difference between Tommy Cat Mikes [the Czech version of, say, Basil Brush] and Milos Jakes?' Answer: 'Tommy Cat Mikes can talk'. This wasn't just agitprop. A pirated tape of Jakes addressing a private party meeting revealed a man of negligible eloquence and limited intellectual grasp. Discussing 'past errors', Jakes said: 'Comrades . . . yes . . . this person [unspecified] made a mistake . . . everyone of us makes mistakes . . . but always . . . who's this Government? . . . when I ask . . . it's a Communist Government . . . Communist. It was, it is, it will be.'

Jokes about Jakes were not approved of. In the early 1980s a Czech wrote a private letter to a friend in West Germany, fantasising about a meeting between Ronald Reagan and Donald Duck. But 'Donald Duck' could have been a coded reference to Jakes, whose name means gander in Czech. This offended against Articles 102 and 103 of the constitution, which proscribe 'defamation of persons holding state office'. Defamation is defined as 'ridiculing, disseminating caricatures, making satirical comments or telling malicious jokes'. The letter writer got two years.

The man who made his name by playing cat and mouse with such Stalinist devices as Articles 102 and 103 in a series of elegant, witty and complex plays, then grew more famous serving a series of prison sentences, was Vaclav Havel, Czechoslovakia's dissident-in-chief. Havel is a gentle, painfully courteous man with a slow, almost arthritic diction and an aversion to the black arts of gesture politics. But his life and his spells in prison – six years in all – schooled him, like no other Czech, to take on the Communist Party with a moral force it completely lacked.

In 1988, more than a year before the revolution, he recalled some of the Kafkaesque absurdities of prison life. His longest spell was from May 1979 to spring 1983, though he was in and out of detention like a jack-in-the-box. In his airy, fourth-floor Prague flat overlooking Hradcany Castle, he remembered the farce of the prison informers – *bonzaks* – coming to him to write their reports on (who else?) Vaclav Havel: 'I had to write many, many confidential reports on myself. I wanted to help the *bonzaks*, and, besides, it was a chance to mystify the authorities.' And with that he blew out some blue cigarette smoke and laughed gently, an utterly improbable revolutionary.

Havel was born in Prague in 1936, two years before Germany moved into Czechoslovakia, and 12 years before Czech Communists, assisted by Moscow, seized the country for themselves. The family was prosperous, thanks to his paternal grandfather, an architect and entrepreneur who put up many splendid Art Nouveau buildings, including the house where Havel has his flat, and other buildings in Wenceslas Square.

A film shot by his father shows him as an expensively dressed baby in a basketwork pram surrounded by pretty women and white-suited men. Most of his life has been a campaign to overcome the alienation and guilt he felt first as a privileged bourgeois child ('a well fed piglet' in his own words) and then, for much longer, when the Communists discriminated against him because of his bourgeois origins.

It was his class which barred him from entrance to university. This ploy of punishing parents by choking off their children's education was a favourite tool for suppressing dissent, right up to the revolution. Instead he joined in 1960 the Theatre on the Balustrade as a stagehand, later to become its presiding spirit. He still writes his plays with this theatre in mind. The seven years at the Balustrade were the happiest of his life. They were the only years his plays could be published and performed in Prague. It was at the theatre that Havel met Jan Patocka, a philosopher ranked by Czechs with Tomas Masaryk, the father of modern Czechoslovakia. The gentle, unassuming Patocka (banned from teaching first by the Nazis and then by the Communists) came to talk at the theatre. 'Listening to Patocka', Havel recalled, 'was bliss'.

Patocka was a true moral philosopher who taught by his life as well as his words. He was to become, in 1977, the founding genius of Charter 77 and, together with Havel and Dubcek's foreign minister Jiri Hajek, its first spokesman. Patocka died two months after the Charter's launching but already Havel had begun to publish – in Czechoslovakia, of course, in samizdat – reflective political essays deeply influenced by his master.

It was this man whose intellectual presence was at Havel's side throughout the revolution, rather than, say, Jaroslav Hasek's *The Good Soldier Svejk* who is often invoked by Westerners seeking to understand how the Czechs coped with repression. In fact, amongst the dissidents, Svejk is something of a dirty word. The dissident and essayist Ludvik Vaculik, another mentor for Havel, wrote in 1984 that Svejk was now in charge of Czechoslovakia, 'applying logic as round as a shaven skull . . . institutionalised incompetence, ignorance armed with full powers'.

The opposition which orbited around Havel also paid homage to the two Masaryks, Tomas, the first President of Czechoslovakia, who ruled benignly over Central Europe's only inter-war democracy and his son Jan, foreign minister in 1948, whose 'suicide' when the Communists wrenched power into their hands looked too convenient to be true.

Intellectually, Communist Party stooges like Jakes were no match for Havel and his friends. But they did not play by the same rules. Havel was continually watched, thumbed over, his every action checked in case any irregularity of personal or civic behaviour should give them cause to lock him up. The secret police even erected a little police box opposite his country cottage, the better to intimidate. Although he was allowed to enjoy a good standard of living – the fruit of foreign performances of the plays his countrymen were not allowed to see – his life was subject to petty, but painful hurts. For example, his IBM computer was one day taken away on a police raid, complete with work in progress: something maddening for a professional writer.

He was picked up on whim. Once the secret police threatened him and added: 'You're a nobody, you know. No-one cares about you'. He returned home to find about 30 foreign journalists standing in the hallway of his flat. President Reagan had mentioned Havel, the secret policeman's nobody, in a speech that very day. Havel's international fame protected him, but lesser known Czechs were not so fortunate. For example, Pavel Wonka, who had tried to stand as an independent candidate against the Communist Party in northern Bohemia, was arrested and imprisoned. While serving his sentence, he died in the spring of 1988. The cause of his death was a blood clot in the groin. The prison authorities denied that Wonka, a healthy young man, had been beaten.

Sometimes the authorities got the better of Havel. After his first spell in prison in the 1970s a written request to be let out was unexpectedly granted; but on the day of his release the press published extracts from his letter which made it appear that he promised to curtail his activities in Charter 77 in exchange for freedom. It was a humiliating coup by the regime, which Havel has never forgotten. The experience toughened him, without destroying his good humour.

Havel's right-hand man through the dead days of prison was his fellow Charter 77 activist Jiri Dienstbier, a Czech journalist who was covering the Vietnam War from Hanoi when the Soviet Union invaded Prague in 1968. In 1988, Dienstbier – no longer a high-flying journalist but a 'stoker' in a mechanised factory, desultorily pushing buttons – claimed that he and Havel went to prison out of laziness. 'It's too tiring to play several different roles. That's the nice thing about being in prison: you don't have to think up a lot of indefensible theories to defend the indefensible.'

Havel spent part of his prison time writing to his wife. His book *Letters to Olga* sets out his philosophical approach: 'I am merely defending my own identity in conditions I did not invent'. The letters are rather sombre in tone, for the following reason: 'When my letters were published in the West, a reader would have thought these letters extremely serious. It made the impression that I had never laughed. Not at all. But the prison governor had forbidden us to make any jokes in our letters, and if you tried, the letter would be censored. So I left all the jokes out.'

Unlike the po-faced, offensively boring idiom of the Party, the opposition under Havel's leadership appreciated the value of humour. As he wrote in his book of essays, *Living in Truth*: 'It seems that in our central European context what is most earnest has a way of blending in a particularly tense manner with what is most comic'.

The opposition out-gunned the Party as far as intellect, integrity and wit were concerned; it also had time on its side. In his six years in prison Havel had plenty of time to dream, to plan, to consider how to work once the pack-ice started to break up and now, on the week beginning Sunday 19 November, the moment – his moment – had finally come.

That Sunday evening, Havel, his friends in Charter 77 and the students formed Civic Forum. Its opening declaration stated that it had been brought about 'on behalf of that part of the Czechoslovak public which is increasingly critical of the present Czechoslovak leadership, and which in recent days has been profoundly shaken by the brutal massacre of peacefully protesting students'. The Forum demanded the immediate resignation of 'discredited' Communists, including Jakes and the Minister of the Interior; the setting up of a committee to investigate the police action; and the release of all prisoners of conscience. The official media made no mention of the founding of Civic Forum, but its monolithic control of information was to collapse the next day.

The demonstration on Monday night was the biggest yet, a vast, snowballing crowd 200,000-strong – according to the state-controlled television channel and CTK, the official news agency. The very fact that the state media reported the crowd meant trouble for the regime; even more ominously, CTK noted that the protesters 'express strong disagreement at the action of the riot police' in breaking up Friday's demonstration. Three newspapers, two of which had been mouth-pieces for the regime's lapdog opposition parties, printed objective accounts of the unrest. The Socialist Party newspaper, *Svobodne Slovo* (*Free Word*) was particularly robust, and printed a statement by the Party leadership condemning the 'police attacks against defenceless demonstrators'. That the Government was clearly losing its leech-like grip on the Czechoslovakian media meant that the rest of the country, hitherto quiet, would begin to realise the scale of the unrest in the capital. Marches, on a much smaller scale, took place in the Slovakian capital Bratislava, Brno, Liberec and other towns. In Teplice, 60 miles north-west of Prague, 8000 demonstrators gathered to protest against air pollution in the North Bohemian coal basin. The crowd denounced the district government, shouting 'No one trusts you any more'.

The V for victory vies with the clenched fist as demonstrators in Wenceslas Square call for change. (Photo: Roger Hutchings)

The Prague demonstration grew in numbers through the day and by around 4.30 pm the square was packed. They swarmed around Wenceslas Square, a longish oblong of about the same size and importance as London's Whitehall, sloping on a gentle ramp up to the National Museum. When the space was filled, the crowd spread upwards: climbing trees, precariously scrambling up scaffolding six storeys high, dancing on top of telephone boxes. The crowd's sense of its power fed on itself, unstoppable.

The chants and banners had real edge now: 'Today Prague, tomorrow the whole country', 'It's the end, Milos', 'Jakes out', 'Jakes in the bin' and, accompanied by the ringing to bells and the jingling of keys, 'Time's up'.

The bells and the keys gave the crowd a fairytale quality. This was literally so, because every Czech children's story – no matter how grim – finishes with a bell ringing and the teller saying 'And that's the end of the story', just as English fairytales invariably begin 'Once upon a time'. Given its size and the years of sinister oppression, there was something magical in the crowd's absence of hate.

After an hour or so of gleeful chanting, the crowd voiced its will: 'To the Castle!' At this, one could almost hear the long, withdrawing roar as power drained from Hradcany Castle – the seat of Czech power from the days of the Jagiellonian kings, the official residence of the Communist President Husak – and flowed into the heart of the crowd.

It moved off from the square, led by two university students carrying the Czech flag, spattered with blood. 'Our friends carried it on Friday', said one. 'It is their blood.' They passed along Narodni Street, the scene of the beatings, shouting 'Free Czechs come with us'. More people tumbled out of buses and trams to swell the crowd. They marched past the scene of what was now known as the 'massacre' where the candles flickered in the dark and came to a stop at the river. On the other side lay the castle, a superb late Gothic monument to Government authority by day, a grimly foreboding place by night, inspiration for Franz Kafka's citadel of fear.

The front ranks of the crowd tore down barricades of corrugated metal, hastily erected by the authorities, which blocked entry to Charles Bridge. The bridge, which has a good claim to be one of the most beautiful river crossings in the world, was also the spot from where a mediaeval saint was thrown into the waters to drown. Happily, history was not repeated. The crowd surged forward, only to be blocked by a wall of riot police. It was the same at every bridge over the Vtlava. At the sight of the police, the crowd chanted 'Jakes' Gestapo, let us through' and 'Murderers', but did not challenge the police with force. One of the crowd asked the police commander: 'Do you realise that the men who gave you your orders have probably done a bunk?' After a short-lived stand-off, the crowd backed away and regathered in the Old Square to fill Prague with anti-Communist noise.

Although immense, the crowd's power lacked shape, clear goals, point. This was promptly provided by Havel, who called a press conference in his flat overlooking the castle from across the river. His ever-present watchers had disappeared and, for once, the press conference went ahead unimpeded. He opened it by remarking: 'The ideals for which I have been struggling for many years and for which I have been imprisoned are beginning to come to life as an expression of the will of the people'. He announced the formation of Civic Forum – the name struck reporters as a close cousin of the successful anti-Communist group in East Germany, New Forum – and declared it was 'an association open to all who wanted democracy in Czechoslovakia'. A journalist asked Havel whether he saw himself as the country's future leader. He replied: 'I would rather be a kingmaker than a king'.

Havel said that coal miners in northern Bohemia had sent him a message that they were going on strike and were urging others to join in, the first such action since 1968, and – Havel did not point out – the very first move in favour of the opposition by a group of workers. The lack of involvement by workers in the protest had worried the opposition; some striking actors, famous for their appearances on television, had set out from Prague to tour provincial factories, explaining the call for a general strike.

The Government went through the old, robotic motions. A spokesman defended Friday's violence: 'We cannot helplessly watch the activities of those groups acting at variance with the Czechoslovak legal order incited from abroad'. Jakes threatened in a speech that 'attempts to manipulate the culture and youth sections' could 'seriously threaten the implementation of necessary changes and lead society into a crisis with unforeseeable consequences'.

To head off those 'unforeseeable consequences', the regime threw into reverse their policy of denying Havel freedom to travel and issued him with a passport to pick up a peace prize in Sweden. Havel, wary of another dirty trick, declined the offer. He said the Government 'would claim that they let a leading dissident travel abroad, and thus try to mask the drastic repressions we are witnessing'.

Havel was not going to be out-foxed. Mischievously, he made a wry call for a new Soviet-led invasion, knowing that the new men in Moscow were probably more on his side than his own Government's. He stirred more trouble by telling reporters that he had received 'feelers' from some members of the Government, though he declined to be precise. Official figures were, he said, 'emulating each other, so as to say they were the first to make contact'. He added that some contacts existed with the Prime Minister, Ladislav Adamec, but would not admit that they had been direct.

The Government was, indeed, beginning to split, between the hardliners, led by Jakes and his right-hand man, Miroslav Stepan, the Prague Party boss, and those inclined to talk to the opposition, led by Adamec, a bluff teddy bear of a man. Stepan was widely held to be an ogre, a view not without supporting evidence. He was one of the very few European politicians outside Romania to visit and heap praise on President Kim Il Sung, whose dynastic Communist dictatorship keeps North Korea wrapped in an Orwellian fog. Stepan was believed to favour a 'Chinese solution' to the unrest, thus guaranteeing that his name would be met with whistles every time the Prague crowd heard it.

The name of Adamec, however, was treated with more respect by the crowd, again not without reason. The day after Bloody Friday two enterprising students from the faculty of journalism rang Adamec's doorbell and spoke to him at home. They described the horrors of Narodni Street. The Prime Minister said that he was simply informed by telephone that the police intervention had been 'mild'. He said he wanted freedom of speech as well, but his speeches were censored by the Communist Party. The students asked him 'Whose fault is the crisis in this country?' After some hesitation, he replied: 'Ours'.

On Tuesday 21 November, a news stand that opened at 5 am sold out in 15 minutes. Three papers, again including *Free Word*, contained details of the strike, the proclamations and the events of the last few days, but police stopped their distribution to the countryside. *Rude Pravo*, the Party newspaper, kept faithful to its usual news values by describing the thousands of protesters who took over the centre of Prague as 'a few people'. It went on to dismiss 'provocations' from 'opportunists and revolutionary petit-bourgeois elements endangering reconstruction'. To read *Rude Pravo*, wrote Michael Simmons of *The Guardian*, was to enter cloud cuckoo land.

Part of the explanation for the Communist Party's immobility in the face of mass protest lay in the scale of the purges after 1968. Jakes, the purger-in-chief, had to get rid of everybody with any sense of political honesty, and that included idealistic Communists too. So, because reform as an option had been erased, the Party, post-1968, was boxed in.

Adamec, considered to be more of a technician than a Party ideologue like Jakes, was the pragmatic exception to this rule. That day, he received a delegation from New Forum made up of a student leader, Martin Mejstrik; Jan Ruml, son of a prominent imprisoned opposition journalist; and a miner, Milan Hruska. The approved communiqué after the meeting made no new noises – it declared that 'socialism was not up for discussion' – but the fact of the meeting was not lost on the protest movement.

The Government was now giving out wildly conflicting signals. The same day that Adamec was playing host to the son of a prisoner, Jakes – the much more powerful figure, and the one with more to lose – made menacing noises in a television broadcast which interrupted regular programmes later that evening. He told viewers: 'There are boundaries which should not be over-stepped', and threatened to 'introduce order'.

Prague had been full of fearful rumours that tanks were approaching the outskirts of the city. University students even warned secondary school children to keep away from the now daily demonstrations at Wenceslas Square. Fears that the secret police would play *agent provocateur* and incite violence swept the crowd. One notice found plastered all over Wenceslas Square that morning called on the students to be violent, a notion in such sharp contrast to the doctrine of peace and love they had been preaching as to lead observers to suspect that they were the work of the men in Bartolomejska Street. The students tore these posters down, and put more of their own up: begging people to be peaceful.

Prague was fast becoming invisible, as every window pane and wall was plastered with posters, cartoons and graffiti. They were as lively as the Government's slogans were ditchwater dull. One showed a farmer in his field, a bubble coming from his glumly set mouth: 'I've always had a lot of crap in my life, but it would be nice to put up with it in a free country'. It was of 1968 vintage; the cartoonist had found his old material matched the new moment. 'Eternal solidarity with the Soviet Union', the Government slogan, did not.

The chants in Wenceslas Square that night featured many old favourites, plus some new variations: 'Dinosaurs resign' and, accompanied by the jangling of perhaps 200,000 sets of keys, 'Give the bells to the clowns'. The speeches, for the first time, came from the balcony of the *Free Word* paper which overlooked the square from about two-thirds of the way down from the National Theatre. From there, Havel, the deputy editor of *Free Word*, and a Catholic priest long banned from his vocation, Fr Vaclav Maly, spoke to the crowd. For the first time, the bulk of the crowd could hear what they were saying, thanks to massive public address loudspeakers, loaned by rock bands. The crowd contained more of a mixture than ever before, even a uniformed policeman who joined in the applause as enthusiastically as everyone else. A message from the Czechoslovakian Roman Catholic Primate, Cardinal Frantisek Tomasek, was read out, in which he called for democracy: 'We cannot wait any more'.

The much loved cardinal made reference to something which had been nagging Czechoslovakian pride – that they were still in the same, dwindling neo-Stalinist camp as Romania and Albania, and not with Poland, Hungary and East Germany; the country was surrounded, he said, by countries 'that had broken the back' of totalitarianism. 'There can be no confidence in the leadership of a state that refuses to tell the people the truth and give them the rights and freedom which are common even in Third World countries'.

Havel's speech was rough-edged, powerful, and showed little trace of his normally tortuously reasoned diction. It received thunderous applause. The evening finished with the pure, crystal voice of Marta Kubisova, a singer banned from singing in public since 1968, leading the crowd in the national hymn. When the hymn had finished there was a moment of stillness as the poignancy of what had happened sunk in; and then a new blast of applause echoed around the square.

The beatings which took place on Bloody Friday, were still, by Wednesday 22 November, the motor of the revolution. A new joke could be heard in the Prague pubs, told by the dozens of people who wore red, white and blue lapel badges, the colours of the Czechoslovak flag which was becoming the symbol of the revolution. What is the beating heart of the Communist Party? Answer: a truncheon. Havel told a young reporter from the *Young World* youth movement newspaper: 'The events of the seventeenth released the safety valve of dissatisfaction in the country'.

Another *Young World* reporter talked his way into the riot police barracks and managed to talk to two of them who took part in Bloody Friday. One was 19, the other 20. They said: 'When the crowd is aggressive the command is: "Go forward using your truncheons", but they are not usually used against women. When they stopped only a few metres from us they started placing candles on the ground. They were sticking flowers behind our shields and into our coats. The candles were meant for us to slip on.

'There are parts of the body we shouldn't hit. Of course, in a given situation, everyone follows his own reason ... an aggressive man slanders you, he touches your shoulder, you want to use your truncheon, you are aiming somewhere, but then something happens and, without you intending it, you hit his head.' And what if the person was lying on the ground? 'Everyone must decide what to do then for himself.'

Dana, another *Young World* reporter, was granted an interview with Jakes. She asked him who was responsible for sending in the riot police. He told her: 'We haven't found out yet'. Such was his response to the burning question of the moment.

The only card left for the authorities to play was force, or the threat of force – the so-called 'Chinese solution'. Stepan did his best to hint at that when he declared that armed units of the People's Militia, the Party's paramilitary force, were standing by. Officers from the so-called People's Militia had been busy ripping down posters calling for the general strike and preventing students, intellectuals and actors from preaching revolution to workers in their factories.

But the question which still worried the opposition was the lack of support from the workers. Some of Pavlina's friends went to one factory in the countryside to lobby for support. They were refused entry by a mistrustful guard. 'You can't come here.' Why not? 'Because you're followers of this fellow Gandhi, and he's in Charter 77, isn't he?' One British reporter went to a pub near the Tatra tram factory in Prague's grey-on-grey industrial suburb of Vysocany. A lot of beer was sunk, but there was little evidence of revolutionary fervour. 'We are worried', said one production line worker. By the police? 'No, about our living.'

By the standards of other Eastern European countries, such as

Members of Civic Forum meet to discuss strategy during the revolution in Czechoslovakia. (Photo: Roger Hutchings)

Poland, the Czechoslovak worker was not badly off at all – a legacy of the country's pre-war economic success. The shops in Prague were well stocked; one butcher's near the Magic Lantern Theatre, the preposterously chic headquarters of the Civic Forum opposition, was, in the words of *The Observer*'s Eastern Europe correspondent, Mark Frankland, 'a mountain of Renoir-pink flesh, an altar to the pig'. As the week wore on, the regime tried to seduce the workers with promises of holidays to exotic places and even flooded the shops with bananas. These were promptly wrapped in patriotic (revolutionary) colours and handed out to the crowd.

The carrot, so to speak, of bananas and the stick of force – even the first snowfall of winter – did nothing to lessen the ardour of the revolutionaries, who gathered for the third day running to block Wenceslas Square. The crowd savoured all the favourite chants and added a new one: 'We want a Government with a higher IQ'. The world's press had by now flooded into Prague to watch the revolution take place, another tip in the balance towards the opposition. In front of the crowd, Havel played superpower politics to the manner born. He announced to cheers that he had sent messages to Presidents Bush and Gorbachov seeking their support.

'Long live Dubcek' was another popular chant, referring to the ousted author of the Prague Spring. After a short spell as the country's Ambassador to Turkey, Dubcek had spent the years since the invasion in a lowly post in Slovakia's Forestry Commission. He had appeared that day in his home town of Bratislava to give support at the show trial of the Catholic activist Jan Czarnogursky, facing a five-year prison sentence on charges of sedition. A message from Dubcek to the Prague crowd was read out, calling for all those in the Communist Party leadership who had helped to crush the Prague Spring to resign. The demonstration itself was for the first time shown live on television.

The following day, Thursday 23 November, the secret police acted to throttle the television coverage. Plainclothes men raided the central television station, sacked the director and installed a deputy Prime Minister, Matej Lucan, in his place. The television staff met and demanded live coverage of the demonstrations and broadcasting of film shot on the night of 17 November; 4900 TV staff supported the demand, with 300 against. The secret police, however, won the argument. A black-edged leaflet on the door of the studios announced: 'We regret to inform you that Czechoslovak television is no longer in the hands of its workers'. But the STB were only partly successful in smothering the opposition's successes; a peculiar form of partial censorship operated for the rest of the week.

Thursday was marked by move and counter-move in the revolutionary chess game. Footballers from the national squad told reporters: 'We support the students ... We have signed the declaration against violence'. They too would strike over the weekend to allow their fans to demonstrate without missing the big matches.

A statement from the Army sided with the Government. Senior Army officers said: 'We reject the anarchy which is spread by external and internal anti-socialist forces'. It expressed support for the Communist Party's efforts to bring 'calm and order' to the situation. But on the ground, the security forces were finding it difficult to realise their words. Units of the People's Militia were said to have ducked orders when faced with the enormity of their task; a riot police unit in one district declared that they no longer wished to be involved in 'solving political problems'; the number of uniformed police officers at Thursday's demonstration was higher than before. The regime's only weapon left was splintering in its hand.

Crucially, the workers in the factories started to swing against the Communist Party. The Prague Party boss, Stepan, attempted to win workers over at the giant CKD engineering works in the city. His discomfort when the crowd whistled him down was televised for the whole nation to see.

Representatives from more than 500 plants and workplaces declared they were backing the demands of the Civic Forum and would come out on strike on Monday. To roars of applause from the crowd in Wenceslas Square a roll-call of pro-opposition factories was read out, including several branches of CKD, the Skoda engineering works, the Tatra heavy engineering and defence group and the Poldi steel works at Kladno. When workers from the Prague CKD plant arrived in the square at about 4 pm, carrying banners and the Czechoslovak national flag, a vast roar of relief was sounded. But the delegation was not a large one.

Havel, his voice croaking from over-use, kept the pressure up in his speech to the crowd: 'No matter what happens in the next few days, we are positive that Monday's general strike will be crucial for the lonesome group of Stalinists who want to hold on to power'. This was a veiled reference to mounting speculation that a specially convened meeting of the ruling Politburo to take place on Friday would sack Jakes. Havel was setting out the opposition's belief that it was not enough for the Communists to be shuffled: the whole deck of cards had to be thrown out.

Havel also made a direct appeal to individual soldiers and members of the People's Militia over the heads of their officers. He told them that they were first and foremost 'human beings and citizens of Czechoslovakia'. As Havel spoke, the crowd booed and hurrahed at mention of its villains and heroes like an English audience at a pantomime. It was vital for the opposition to show the Politburo, which was holding an extraordinary meeting the next day, that it still had control of its people power. The crowd gave a stunning performance of disciplined disobedience towards the Government: there was even a high-wire, anti-Communist act. One man hung like a spider in the middle of a defunct neon sign high above the crowd; miraculously, he did not fall off.

In Bratislava, Dubcek addressed another large crowd, after a court in the Slovak capital cleared Jan Czarnogursky of the sedition charges. Dubcek, speaking in public for the first time since the Soviet tanks silenced him, said: 'Man is the important thing, and there is no socialism without proper living conditions'. He said that there had been no progress in the last 20 years, but warned against making extreme demands that could have 'tragic consequences'.

He was being too pessimistic. The following evening, Friday 24 November, Dubcek appeared in person in front of the Prague crowd, packed like sardines in Wenceslas Square. His gentle smile shone like a beacon as he told the crowd: 'I am among you again', and made as if to embrace the whole nation by holding out his arms and then bringing them to his chest. He went on: 'Again I raise my voice and call for a renewal of society'. The crowd answered back: 'Dubcek, Dubcek, Dubcek'. He carried on: 'We lived for a long time in the darkness. Now it is the dawn. We must unite in one movement to build a free Czechoslovakia.' He went on to admonish the security forces: 'Don't be traitors to your people'.

*

A few hours later, as Dubcek and Havel were giving a Civic Forum press conference in the Magic Lantern Theatre the news broke that Jakes and the entire Politburo, which had spent all day closeted together in a crisis meeting, had resigned. The two men fell into each other's arms. 'I think', said the playwright, 'it is time for champagne'. Later that night, it is said, Havel and his friends went to their favourite pub and wallowed in an evening of laughter and beer.

In the square, the people of Prague were catapulted into ecstasy, a joy heightened by the fear which had gone before. Taxis raced around the square with horns blaring, and a brass band in one corner oompahed out an end to four decades of Communism. Nearby, a non-musician blew a trumpet, horribly out of tune. It didn't matter. They danced and sang and kissed each other. 'We're free', they said, 'we're free'. The Party had been flipped over, like the man-insect in Kafka's *Metamorphosis*: 'He was lying on his hard, as it were armour-plated, back ... His numerous legs, which were pitifully thin compared to the rest of his bulk, waved helplessly before his eyes.'

Jakes had given way to Karel Urbanek, an unknown, whose only real qualification for office was his obscurity. Others of the old guard, including Stepan, were still on the Politburo. So it was not a clear-cut victory. There were a few jagged edges left of the Party, but its nerve had snapped. Concrete evidence of the stupefaction of the Government was produced when a press conference at the Inter-Continental Hotel for the vast hordes of foreign journalists was repeatedly put back; finally, a Party spokesman emerged to utter gobbledegook at 3 am on Saturday morning. The journalists gave the Party spokesman a none-too-gentle roasting, not least because they had been kept from their beds.

The feverishness of the past few days gave way to a calmer, elegiac mood when Cardinal Tomasek, who suffered severely at the hands of the regime in the 1950s, presided over Mass in St Vitus Cathedral. Ostensibly the Mass was to honour the canonisation of St Agnes of Bohemia in Rome; it turned out to be a thanksgiving service for the revolution. A more secular thanksgiving took place at Prague Airport, when the protest singer Jaroslav Hutka, exiled for 12 years, returned home. Before he was allowed through customs, he could be seen through a glass wall. He took up his guitar and started to sing; his friends, who could not hear him through the glass, started singing in unison.

On Saturday, the site of the daily demonstration switched to Letna Park, where 500,000 people heard speeches from Dubcek and Havel. The latter read a strong statement by Civic Forum belittling the new Politburo and described Monday's general strike as an 'informal referendum' on Communist Party rule. The unloved Stepan, shortly after he had been re-elected to the Politburo, had resigned after a further meeting of the Prague Communist Party. But Havel did not concede an inch: 'We are receiving verified reports proving that the new leadership of the Party is just a trick and that the instruments of power are being taken over by neo-Stalinists'. The showman in him came to the fore as his speech climaxed: 'The time is at hand', hc shouted. The crowd, responding in one voice, roared back: 'It is here!'

The next day, Sunday 26 November, a newly opened advice centre was besieged by people, including a madman claiming that the Central Committee had planted a device in his head which was now controlling him.

Sunday's daily rally, again held at Letna Park, had the mood of an epilogue. Three riot policemen, in uniform, appeared to plead forgiveness for their colleagues who had beaten up the students on Bloody Friday. Petr Uhl, newly released from prison, apologised to the people for misleading them about the 'death' of Martin Smid. Again, given the smudging of lives, the sustained, sophisticated cruelty of the regime, the crowd's magnanimity was striking. After Dubcek, Havel and Jiri Ruml – also sprung from prison – had spoken, Marta Kubisova led the people in the national anthem. The crowd, which was beginning to drift off, stopped dead to listen.

The next day the nation stopped work to the din of church bells, even the taxi drivers, who blocked Prague's ring road in a two-mile ribbon of cars. The implosion of the Communist Party, now tumbling into an abyss of disarray, gave the general stike an air of anti-climax. everyone joined in; it was, after all, now completely safe to do so.

Czechoslovak soldiers join the celebrations in Prague after the fall of the Government. (Photo: Roger Hutchings)

The days that followed were a time of gentle reckoning. This took place across the country, in all walks of life, at high level and low. But nobody died. A few – including former Prague Communist Party chief Stepan – were arrested and charged with crimes of inciting violence against the people. In Dr Pelant's faculty, one of the scientists owed his job and his superiority to his Party card. The faculty held a staff meeting, in which the Party man changed the tune he had been whistling for so long. He made a long speech, attacking the errors of the Party and finished up chanting 'Husak, resign, Husak, resign!' He chanted so loudly it was as if he had been in a crowd, not at a faculty meeting. No one joined him in his chanting. When he had finished, there was a long, empty silence.

The daily rallies were stopped after the Monday of the general strike; the revolutionaries went home, slept for days, and tried to recover from their liberation influenza, many unsure of the great victory they had won. Their confidence was fragile, and rightly so.

The new Government was announced on 3 December. To Civic Forum, it looked very much like a stooge one, with only five non-Communists in a 20-man Cabinet. The following day, 300,000 people packed Wenceslas Square to bellow their sense of betrayal. The Communists trembled, and then capitulated. Prime Minister Ladislav Adamec tried to play honest broker between the Communist rearguard and Civic Forum, but found it impossible to bear the strain. On 7 December he resigned.

People hungry for information grab leaflets handed out in Prague. (Photo: Roger Hutchings)

Three days later, less than a month after the revolution had started, a new Government with a majority of non-Communists was sworn in, elected by the Communists' shame-faced Parliament. After the swearing-in had taken place, President Husak himself resigned. The new Government's Foreign Minister was Havel's old cellmate, Jiri Dienstbier; in charge of the Interior Ministry, including, of course, the secret police, was Jan Czarnogursky, who had been their reluctant guest in custody only days before. After some jostling within Civic Forum, a new speaker of the Czech Parliament was proposed: Alexander Dubcek. He had expressed a desire to become President, and there was much love for the man's simple grace and humanity, but his faithfulness to socialism as an ideal ruled him out as a contender.

Husak's successor, who promised to oversee free elections in the new year, was elected on the last day but one of 1989. His name was Vaclav Havel.

ROMANIA
The half-finished revolution

19 March 1965	Georghe Gheorghiu-Dej, First Secretary of the Communist Party dies; Nicolai Ceausescu replaces him.
15 November 1987	Thousands of workers protest in Brasov against pay; Ceausescu puts down unrest.
16–17 December 1989	Parishioners of Father Laszlo Tokes gather around his church in Timisoara to protest over his removal; march broken up by force.
21 December 1989	Ceausescu shouted down as he speaks in Bucharest; security forces fire on crowds, killing many.
22 December 1989	Army switches sides; Ceausescus flee; Securitate fights back. Fighting continues for four days.
23 December 1989	National Salvation Front declares itself in charge.
25 December 1989	Nicolai and Elena Ceausescu put on trial, convicted and executed by firing squad.
May 1990	Free elections promised.

It is a name, but it sounds like a slogan. You still hear it everywhere, at every gathering that is remotely political. It is made to be shouted out, a four-syllable sound that was once just the name of a town but became a rallying cry for a whole country. It echoed all over Romania for the 10 days of revolution, and reverberated through the centre of Bucharest for the dramatic 10 hours that changed everything. It begins with a vicious, spitting noise, goes on with a dangerous rumble and ends with a harsh, ravaged sound that should be yelled out. TI-MI-SHA-RAAA!

Timisoara is an unlikely town to have changed history. Like everywhere else in Romania, it is numbingly poor. Its medieval centre is crumbling and its anonymous new apartment blocks, hurriedly built to house the villagers that the old regime had forced out of their homes, were in need of repair before they were even completed. Once a centre of learning, when it was part of Hungary, it is the kind of bleak town you want to forget as soon as you have passed through it.

Nobody will forget it now. Its population may be largely ethnic Hungarians, traditionally distrusted, disliked even, by native Romanians, but they are all heroes now, especially the dead ones. Along with the universal rallying cry there are always banners with the name 'Timisoara' written on them. It is scrawled on bullet-pitted walls in Bucharest, lines of red dripping from each of its nine letters to represent blood.

Romania's revolution was altogether different. This was the country seemingly unaffected by the months of change in Eastern Europe. While other nations were falling over themselves to change their way of life, Party chiefs bowing to the will of the people, governments disappearing almost without a struggle, Romania remained unchanged.

It won its freedom the hard way, in a bloody, vicious, spectacular and historic battle that nobody had anticipated, nobody had even seriously fantasised about. It was a battle that nobody who saw it will ever forget, not just for the level of violence, but also for a curious, exhilarating, freewheeling, ecstatic quality.

Its drama was the stuff of history: the central area in Bucharest, the Palace Square containing both the old palace and the new palace, the Party headquarters, in flames; people crowding round tanks urging the soldiers on; old ladies bringing freshly baked bread to the Army, whose tanks were covered with cheering people. Phrases were shouted aloud that in other circumstances would have sounded mawkish but here thrilled the soul – 'You may kill us, but we won't go away'. Tracer bullets crossed the sky like celebratory fireworks, while the rattle of automatic fire from security forces, the 'bandits', was continuous. There was panic as bandits merged with the crowds in plain clothes, pulling out guns and starting to shoot indiscriminately; elation as people waved the Romanian flags, all with holes in the middle where the Communist Party symbol had been torn out; noise as they cheered, shouted, jeered and screamed; silence as people fell dead. From buildings all over the city, snipers opened fire, aiming indiscriminately at young and old. Lorry-loads of young people, commandeering every available vehicle, roared up and down the boulevards, daring, taunting the snipers, shouting hitherto banned works like 'Liberty', 'Democracy', 'Freedom', and the inevitable 'Ti-mi-sha-raaa'. Some of these vehicles lay abandoned by the kerb, riddled with bullets and stained with blood. Everywhere was the raised two-finger salute of people's power. It needed a Goya to paint the scenes. The television cameras captured the events but not the excitement.

After it had started, the momentum seemed unstoppable and victory inevitable. But all over the country there are now graves and carefully tended memorials, their eternal flames replenished by candles from relatives and passers-by, loaves of bread and even packets of cigarettes littering their bases, given as traditional offerings. These are the reminders that freedom came, like the repression before it, out of the barrel of a gun.

After the fighting was over and people tried to work out what had actually started it all, there was speculation that Romania had not undergone a people's revolution so much as a *coup d'état*, that the whole thing had been planned in advance. This speculation was false – the attempt to seize political power was yet to come. It is possible that some dissidents had discussed secretly what they could do to overthrow Ceausescu, but it was more fantasy than planning. What the world saw in Romania in December 1989 was nothing less than a popular uprising, a spontaneous overflow of powerful and unstoppable feeling. 'Romania was like a great glass with water full to the brim', explained one demonstrator. 'We could not take any more.'

The political chaos and distrust that still linger in the aftermath of the revolution are equally grim reminders that the struggle for democracy is a war, not just a battle. The December revolution in Romania – 22 December is the new National Day – may have rid the country of a political black hole, but it has yet to replace it with anything else. The overthrow of Ceausescu has pushed Romania into an exciting but unfamiliar state of liberty. 'We don't know what freedom means', explained one student. 'We don't know how to use freedom. We don't know what it is to walk, to talk and to think free. We have only seen darkness and silence.' Romania still faces political crisis, fought not with words rather than bullets. After the sacrifices they had made over Christmas, people somehow expected everything to be immediately better, as if all the country's problems would be solved by the execution of Nicolai and Elena Ceausescu. It couldn't be: the legacy of decay was too great. Ceausescu called his rule 'The Era of Light', but everywhere there was darkness.

If you had drawn up a blueprint for a country in Eastern Europe where revolution was logically impossible, you would have found yourself describing Romania. There was, for a start, no organised opposition to the ruling Communist Party, no New Forum, no Civic Forum, no writers and intellectuals meeting in tiny garrets to plot and plan. There were no Havels, no Walesas, no heroes, no symbols, no natural leaders. The few people who had dared in March to write Nicolai Ceausescu a very gentle protest letter – couched in safe Marxist rhetoric and urging the maintenance of a Communist regime – were all under house arrest. So, too, was the former high ranking diplomat who had compiled a report on human rights' abuses.

By law, all typewriters had to be registered with the authorities, together with a copy of their typeface, making the circulation of clandestine pamphlets impossible. There were no photocopiers or duplicating machines. There had been no gatherings, meetings or discussion groups as there were in other Eastern countries. One in four of the population was estimated to be an informer, often under threat or intimidation. Even if this statistic was exaggerated, it was a fearful and efficient rumour and people were unwilling to put its veracity to the test. The infrastructure of organised dissent was impossible. Meetings with foreigners were not actually forbidden, but any conversation had to be reported to the authorities within 24 hours, and the inevitable interrogation and subsequent harassment was more than enough to put most people off.

The feared secret police, the Securitate, tapped telephones at will and harassed people almost at random and with awesome bureaucratic efficiency. People vanished without trace, even, on occasions, foreigners staying at the Intercontinental Hotel where every room was bugged and the staff was riddled with informers. Nobody knew how many political prisoners were in the jails, or even what constituted a political crime. A young medical student whose only crime was to study yoga was not only beaten up by the Securitate and ordered to desist, but the organisation found enough manpower to have four separate men follow her to and from the university. Her mental and spiritual activities were deemed political. If a political crime could not actually be proved, then people were imprisoned as alleged homosexuals, or put into prison hospitals as mental cases. Communist Party chiefs at every factory had files on all workers, listing any forbidden and dangerous show of individuality. The workers at a tractor factory in Brasov who had downed tools in 1987 in protest at the extreme cold had either been imprisoned or sent into exile in distant parts of Romania. One woman whose husband had disappeared complained frequently to the authorities; she was told he was at home. When she said this was demonstrably untrue she was told he was on 'unpaid leave'. Romania refused to sign international human rights' declarations, saying that its human rights were already fully safeguarded.

People were too cold, too tired from queuing all day for food, too exhausted from the practical struggle to survive, to have enough time or will to consider ideas like freedom. Even though Romania has the second largest national flock of sheep in Europe (after Britain) there was no meat in the shops; people queued for hours and found nothing but a sheep's head when they finally got to the counter. Everything was going for export; Ceausescu was clearing all his foreign debts, so that no outsider would be able to tell him what to do, or put pressure on him to change his policies.

Monuments to his methods abound. They range from the vast Palace of the Republic in Bucharest – hundreds of historic old buildings were summarily demolished to create space for it and the Victory of Socialism Boulevard – to a power plant at Anina that cost more than $1 billion to build but is incapable of producing any electricity. Agricultural production figures were overestimated by up to 400 percent. When a foreign businessman told the dictator that he had seen no meat in the shops, Ceausescu said this was because Romanians kept it at home in their deep freezes. The authorities even used to lie about the weather forecast: it never officially dropped below 50 degrees, even when there was deep snow on the ground, because the law said that heating had to be turned on if it did.

Although Romania was a major producer and exporter of drugs and antibiotics, medical supplies were almost non-existent. The official food and medicines meant to last a child for six months lasted that many weeks and if a family could not bribe a doctor or a nurse, the child suffered. Children were not registered until they were six months old, in an attempt to keep the infant mortality figures down. After the revolution, it was discovered that over 350 children and babies in Romania's hospitals had Aids or were HIV-positive. Their mothers were negative; the infection had come from contaminated blood and dirty needles. Ceausescu had boasted that Romania was free from Aids, and the children had been kept secret for fear of proving his boast wrong. It seemed no accident that Vlad Dracula had lived in Romania; centuries later the country was still the land of the living dead.

Because of all this, it seemed that the winter of content that was sweeping across Eastern Europe would pass Romania by. The Iron Curtain had not come down, just shifted. While Hungary threw open its frontiers, Romania closed its yet more tightly. Romanian television was heavily censored; one documentary maker was ordered to make

27 cuts in a 30-minute programme. Nicolai used to ring up in the middle of a programme if there was something he didn't like and pretty girls were forbidden to appear because his wife did not like them. Yet Romanians discovered what was happening among their neighbours from the television stations of Hungary, Yugoslavia, the Soviet Union, and Bulgaria, and from the BBC and Radio Free Europe. Watching or listening in secret, the Romanians must have felt they were living in an island of repression.

But the leadership of Romania was also aware of what was happening in the rest of Europe. Ominously, the official media kept reminding the people what Romania's friend and ally, China, had done so effectively in Tiananmen Square to quell an uprising. Socialism must not be betrayed, said Ceausescu as he made a speech to the Party conference in November, condemning the changes in the East and warning that they must not, would not, happen here. The Party faithful gave him 67 standing ovations. The rest of the country stayed silent.

And then Timisoara erupted. It began as a local issue, one that did not even involve the whole area. A young pastor, Laszlo Tokes, had been told earlier in the summer by his Church, ever fearful of standing up to the Government, that he was to be moved to another area of Romania. His sermons and the concern he had expressed at the Government's treatment of the 1.7 million ethnic Hungarians were proving troublesome. Rumours spread that he was to be moved on the weekend of 16–17 December and a few of his parishioners began to gather in front of his church, both as a silent protest and just to say farewell.

The crowd grew, encircling the church, as the protest gathered momentum. Most of the demonstrators were young. The next few days in Romania were to show that Ceausescu had, quite literally, sowed the seeds of his own destruction. For many years he had banned birth control and made abortions illegal. Intent on raising the population from 22 million to 30 million he had created a huge army of dissatisfied young people. They were known as 'Ceausescuites'.

Nobody was planning a revolt, let alone a revolution, in Timisoara; but the authorities were unused to any kind of dissent, untrained in crowd control. They were faced with a crowd of several thousand, some linking hands to surround the church with a symbolic human fence, others just milling around. Instead of breaking up the crowd with riot police and even tear gas, they brought in the Army.

The Romanian Army is made up largely of conscripts and their usual jobs include domestic chores like helping bring in the harvest and clearing city streets of snow. Firing their guns at all, let alone firing them at their own countrymen, was a new experience. But within the Army, modelled on its Russian counterpart, are divisions of

Mourners at a village funeral for a young girl killed by gunfire. (Photo: Dod Miller)

Securitate, identifiable by different flashes on their uniforms, who ensure the soldiers obey orders. Those orders were to shoot the protesters. It was an order that was obeyed with savage dedication.

The locals nickname for the centre of Timisoara is now 'Red Square', not, of course, out of any deference to Moscow but because it was stained with dried blood for days. The shooting was fierce; helicopters were brought in and and the Securitate fired from them as well. Children and women were shot. When the people returned the next day crying 'Give us our dead', the Army opened fire again, killing yet more. But the crowds still came back, braving the guns to yell and jeer at the troops. It was not to be another Brasov, a brief show of defiance and resentment that was quickly stamped out, punished and almost forgotten. If, in Camus's description, 'a rebel is a man who says no', then all the people of Timisoara became rebels that weekend. Their acquiescence snapped. They shouted no.

Urban terror breeds urban myths. Awful and awesome rumours about the number of those dead and injured in Timisoara spread rapidly throughout the country and the world. The authorities sealed the town off, allowing nobody in, expelling foreigners and ordering the international trucks to take another route to the frontiers with Hungary and Yugoslavia. A state of emergency was declared in the town and the surrounding area. But still the news and the rumours spread – 2000, 4000, 10,000 dead. Eyewitness accounts from the unreliable eyes of departing foreigners spoke of mass slaughter in Timisoara on an unimaginable scale, of trucks taking bodies away and of mass graves being dug. There were claims that soldiers had refused to fire on the crowds, and had been shot in turn by their Securitate colleagues. Lorries were said to have arrived in the middle of the night to dispose of the bodies in mass graves or by hasty cremation. Even normally cautious sources like the US embassy in Bucharest were saying that they had no exact figures for the death toll but there was 'no doubt that a massacre has taken place'. It was later to become clear that the figures for the dead in Timisoara were hideously exaggerated, as indeed they later were for the whole of the country. Some of the corpses dug from mass graves were in fact earlier victims of state torture. The actual figure for the dead in Timisoara would turn out to be 'only' about 100. But who knows, if the true and accurate figure had been available at the time, large as it is, it might not have been large enough to rouse a country finally to wrath. Even the mythical dead did not die in vain.

As the news spread, so did the discontent, with crowds gathering everywhere. No mention of Timisoara was made in the official newspapers, which contented themselves with news of Nicolai Ceausescu's visit to Iran (the only other newspapers not to carry any news of the rumoured massacre were those of China). The two and a half hours of state television shown in the evening were still full of news about wheat harvests and tractor production, with nothing about Timisoara. Romanian diplomats abroad reassured Western governments that there had been no protest and that human rights were safe in Timisoara. But the Government nevertheless declared a state of emergency in most of Transylvania and there were troops in every Romanian town curbing demonstrations. In Bucharest they guarded Government buildings, factories and the television station. But still Ceausescu did not panic. Perhaps because revolt was so unthinkable, he did not think about it. Instead, he left for his state visit to Iran to negotiate a trade deal, leaving his wife Elena, the First Deputy Prime Minister, in charge of the country with instructions to maintain order no matter how.

After that weekend, the country was in a state of uneasy tension. Ceausescu returned from Iran and announced that everything was now calm in the country, although he did acknowledge that there had been civil disturbances 'in Timisoara and elsewhere'. He announced an increase in the minimum wage, as if that was all the unrest had been about. The official Romanian news agency, Agerpres, described the weekend's carnage in Timisoara as 'the serious violation of public order in the Timisoara district through acts of terrorism, vandalism and destruction of public assets'. There was no mention of crowds chanting 'Give us our dead', or of the group of people shot as they walked to the local Party headquarters to argue against the removal of Pastor Tokes.

Then Ceausescu made a series of political blunders that effectively lost him his power and, ultimately, his life. Misreading the signs, and believing misleading advice given him by sycophantic ministers who feared his wrath if they displeased him, he went on the offensive. On Wednesday 20 December, he made a speech blaming all the troubles in Timisoara and elsewhere on the traditional bugbears, 'foreign agents, hooligans, fascists and traitors'. Understandably, this enraged the country. In the towns where there had been disturbances, and where people had been killed, passions were inflamed. 'They were our children who were killed', said an old lady from Arad, 'how dare he call them traitors?'

But still Ceausescu might have survived. The flames of revolt were burning in Romania, but they still could have been snuffed out: they were not yet a forest fire. Ceausescu thought he could do what the other Eastern European governments had been fearful of doing: gamble everything on his ability to maintain iron control of his troops and security forces while using them to put down huge public demonstrations by force. Without Soviet tanks to back them up – with Gorbachov, indeed, urging them not to use force – all the other governments chose peaceful accommodation. But Ceausescu believed that, even without Soviet support, he could maintain himself by the rule of the gun forever. For the first few days of the uprising, it looked as if he might be right. With no political opposition and no independent legal structure, there would have been no post-mortems, no calls for a revaluation or an inquiry. There would have been purges and punishments, and the Government would have become even more repressive. But it would have survived. It was never a Government that set out to court popularity.

Then came the great blunder, the biggest mistake of all. Having ignored the people for so long, Ceausescu felt confident enough to ignore all the signs and to believe his own myth. On Thursday 21 December he decided to hold one of his carefully contrived spontaneous demonstrations of support in front of Party headquarters, on live television, to let the population know he was still in command. For years, he had officially sanctioned a personality cult of extraordinary dimensions. The roads of Romania were littered with mock temples proclaiming the name of Ceausescu. In the centre of Bucharest was a megalomaniac's museum containing endless rooms full of the presents and honours bestowed on him and his wife. The knighthood from the Queen was there, as was the honorary doctorate from the Central London Polytechnic awarded to his wife (even though someone else used to write her scientific papers). So too were pointless trinkets picked up on foreign visits, castanets from Spain, and worthless souvenirs like the honorary citizenship of Texas. Now, Ceausescu decided, was the time to assert his personality.

From early Thursday morning, factory workers were bussed in from all around Bucharest to assemble in front of the balcony of the Party buildings. As usual they were given flags to wave and banners to hold. As usual, they were ordered to cheer.

But this was not to be a usual day. From Timisoara there came the strange rumour that soldiers had turned up in the main square on tanks carrying white flags. It later became clear that the Defence Minister, Vasile Milea, had tried to order troops not to fire on unarmed civilians, but this was not known at the time. (Milea died that day – the official explanation was suicide, but he was in fact shot for this act of disobedience.) There were also rumours that the Securitate were again shooting both at civilians and at the mutinous soldiers. Some students at Bucharest University, brave and with a sense of humour, had hung pears from the branches of apple trees, an ironic reference to the speech that Ceausescu had made at the Party conference, when delegates applauded him as he said that Romania would begin to change its policies only when pears began to grow on apple trees.

Amidst all this whispered confusion, the 71-year-old dictator made his appearance on the balcony. A small man, only his head and shoulders appeared over the parapet, a benign smile on his face as he looked down at the silent crowd beneath him. Taking their silence for support, he waved and began to speak. But almost before he started, he was forced to stop as a woman's scream filled the air. It was soon followed by sporadic but fierce shouting from a large group of students and workers standing at the side of the square. 'Killer', they yelled, 'Timisoara'. It was almost possible, almost, to feel sorry for Nicolai Ceausescu at that moment. The television cameras captured his face looking frail and puzzled at this unexpected response from the crowd. He smiled at first, and waved uncertainly in the direction of the noise as if it were the usual, mechanical shouts of approval. As the noise grew and grew, his expression changed to bewilderment, his face lost any semblance of authority and he suddenly looked very old indeed. A look of terror flickered across his face as two bodyguards stepped forward to usher him from the vulnerable balcony. The television screens across the country went blank.

The crowd in the square seemed just as astonished. What they had just done may be normal behaviour in the West; but by Romanian standards it was bravery beyond belief. Many workers who had made up the official enforced audience had by now begun shouting and many had thrown down their banners and trampled on them. They joined the other group and in a mood of uncertainty the crowd slowly left the square. The protest had been unplanned, and nobody had any idea what to do next. 'We knew there was no going back, but we didn't know how to go forward', recalled one student later.

Ceausescu had spoken at midday. Throughout the afternoon, nothing much happened. Crowds gathered and dispersed. But by the evening a large crowd had gathered in the square outside the university in the heart of the city, in front of the Intercontinental Hotel. Troops watched the crowd for hours, doing nothing as it got bigger and bigger.

Then the killing began. Doctors and nurses who watched the massacre from a window overlooking the city's central University Square said the shooting began at 10.30 pm after a prolonged stand-off between security forces and unarmed students. With the students silhouetted by spotlights from nearby buildings, Securitate forces opened fire at close range with machine guns. Many fell dead or injured as the shooting started, and several hundred others started running for cover. 'Then the security men went in among the wounded and started bayoneting them and butting them with their guns', said Tonescu Aurelia Lucia, a nurse from nearby Coltea Hospital. She watched the killings from a fourth-floor window. 'There were also snipers on the roof of nearby buildings and they shot many protesters in the back.' Most of the 85 civilians that the hospital treated for gunshot wounds had been shot in the back.

After the shooting stopped at 11.45 pm, covered military trucks were quickly driven to the square. The security men who had shot the protesters hurriedly loaded the bodies, each of which was carefully stripped of its identity card before being tossed into the trucks. The bodies have still not been found. Street-cleaning machines were then dispatched to the area to wash away the blood. A British diplomat drove through the area early on Friday morning while the cleaning machines were still in operation; when he got back to the embassy the tyres of his car were red. The only visible evidence of the massacre remaining by Friday morning were large brownish stains of dried blood in subway entrances near the square. The glass front to the Intercontinental Hotel was smashed and the bullet marks along nearby walls were all at body height. A few score protesters managed to flee to the nearby hospital, where they were hidden by doctors and nurses. A nurse said she later saw two of the protesters shot to death – in the back – as they tried to sneak away from the hospital in the middle of the night. 'It was like some kind of nightmare, what I have seen. The bodies were piled into trucks and made to disappear. In the morning the streets were cleaned to look normal', recalled a nurse.

Friday 22 December was a day of revolution and counter-revolution. It was a day of confusion when the battle swung first one way, then the other. As dawn broke, Ceausescu appeared to have clung to power, thanks to the bloody massacre of the previous night. Throughout the country, crowds of people gathered in towns to confront the Army and its Securitate masters. 'We stood in the square on Friday morning waiting to die', recalled a resident of Brasov. People began to assemble again in front of Bucharest University, in the same place where the guns had mowed down their friends in the midnight hours. Troops in tanks and armoured personnel carriers approached down the main, wide boulevard and stopped about 50 yards away. There seemed to be no Securitate forces with them. For hours, there was a tense stand-off, and then a soldier stood up on a tank in full view of the crowd and removed the magazine from his automatic rifle. Other soldiers did the same. Either they had finally heard of the order from their late chief not to fire, or they were aware of the late night bargaining by officials that took place on Thursday – or they too just could not take it anymore.

The crowd began to yell 'The Army is with us' and advanced on the tanks. They clambered all over them, shoved the branches of Christmas trees down the barrels of the guns, and embraced the soldiers. Then the raggle-taggle procession turned round and began to march towards the Palace Square. Shouting and yelling with nervous exhilaration, they urged passers-by to join the revolution. The crowds and the enthusiasm swelled. When the people came in sight of the Party headquarters, and marched towards the balcony from which Ceausescu had spoken the previous day, officials began to pour out of

The Army takes the people's side: tanks in Bucharest as smoke rises from burning buildings. (Photo: Dod Miller)

the building, running away from the crowd. There was some firing from within the building, originating from Securitate men rather than soldiers, but the crowd pressed forward, reached the doors and the braver ones rushed in. Inside, they found pandemonium and fear as officials desperately tried to burn documents and escape. Fuelled by rage, excitement and an onrush of adrenalin as they began fully to realise what was happening, the crowd went in search of their old leaders. On the third floor, hiding in a tiny room, they found the head of the Securitate. He was armed, but a young medical student with an unloaded gun managed to bluff him into surrendering. Students rushed out on to the balcony and began to yell jubilantly to the crowd that the seat of power was in their hands.

But there was no sign of Nicolai and Elena Ceausescu. As the crowd milled around the building, the couple were escaping in undignified panic. So many people crowded into the lift taking them to the roof that others were forced to run up the stairs. As the first pursuers finally emerged on to the flat roof, they were greeted by the sight of a helicopter taking off. Nicolai was sitting on the co-pilot's lap, and a bodyguard had a pistol at the pilot's head. The helicopter flew off unsteadily.

What followed was an uneasy and bewildered calm. Reports came in from all over the country that soldiers had symbolically laid down their arms, and that nobody was fighting. The news from Bucharest that the Ceausescus had fled spread across the country. Slowly, a people unused to celebrating began to celebrate. Troops took over the television and radio stations. Romanian flags began to appear with the hated Communist symbol in the middle torn out. Small groups of young people paraded up and down the streets, shouting and waving. People in cars began to give the two-fingered victory salute of people power. Dissidents were released from prison or from house arrest, and a hastily gathered group of them went to the television station to broadcast messages to the country, their ideas written on scraps of paper and the backs of envelopes, giving an early glimpse of the political chaos that was to follow. One large group declared themselves the National Salvation Front. Their first act was to declare that Christmas would be a holiday – for the first time in 43 years – their second to announce that free multi-party elections would be held, also for the first time in 43 years.

People did not, however, flock on to the streets in huge numbers. Most people were too unused to celebration, too instinctively fearful and too habitually downtrodden to react enthusiastically. But everything was calm enough to believe that indeed Ceausescu had been overthrown. If there had been a free press, its afternoon editions would have carried the headline: 'Ceausescu overthrown! Romania celebrates after 24 years of dictatorship'. By early evening, a hastily duplicated single sheet newsletter was indeed being handed out at street corners. Its headline read simply 'Liberty!'

The celebrations were premature. At about 7 pm, a dramatic counter-revolution began. Not all the Army had gone over to the people; the troops were no longer attacking, but many Army leaders had held their hand, keeping their troops in barracks and waiting to see who would be the victor. Ceausescu was still at large. Securitate forces had been gathering in Bucharest and in cities all over the country, using vast hidden networks of underground tunnels. Of the 45,000 people employed by Securitate, many were simple bureaucrats filling out the requisite forms needed to torture someone or tap their phones, but about 20,000 were fighters. Most of them were busy trying to flee the revenge of their neighbours and the wrath of their countrymen, but the elite corps, the Fifth Directorate, knew no other loyalty than to Ceausescu. They knew their life was finished if Ceausescu were not in power. Many had been taken from orphanages at an early age, indoctrinated in the dictator's ideology and taught to regard Nicolai and Elena as their parents, so that they would protect them at all costs.

It was this group that decided to fight, using 'Plan M', a top secret strategy to create panic, confusion and terror by the indiscriminate and wanton killing of innocent civilians. There were later claims that many of these murderers were in fact 'foreign agents', notably Libyans and Palestinians from the training camps outside Bucharest. There

A Romanian soldier looks anxiously for Securitate snipers firing from windows in Bucharest. (Photo: Dod Miller)

were even allegations that Ceausescu had brought back an elite group of commandos with him from Iran. These rumours were reported as facts, as if the Romanians were unwilling to believe that their fellow countrymen could do such things. Nobody produced any 'foreign' captives and when the fighting was finally over, the allegations ceased. Like the death toll of Timisoara, it was a useful myth. The killers were Romanian.

They began the slaughter in Bucharest in a mixture of frenzy and selectivity. Emerging from the network of tunnels into the Palace Square, they hid in nearby buildings and began to fire at the Central Party headquarters, and at the crowds who had gathered. The captured head of the Securitate broadcast an order to his men to lay down their arms, but they ignored him. They had nothing left to lose, and everything to gain if they could restore the Ceausescu regime to power. They occupied houses surrounding the other key buildings in Bucharest, the radio and television stations, and began shooting. The labyrinth of secret passages even enabled them to get inside these buildings and fight pitched battles in the corridors. Radio and television would first broadcast appeals for people to go to these crucial posts, then it would follow up with appeals for them to stay away. The Army returned fire, setting alight the University Library in the Palace Square next to Securitate headquarters. The Palace itself, with its collection of rare paintings, was ablaze. People cheered as they watched these battles, and some died as the snipers claimed victims.

It could be argued that there was a strategy in the Securitate attacks on these key buildings, a coherent military purpose. But no such logic can be applied to the occupation of random buildings all over the city and the indiscriminate shooting of passers-by from rooftops. This had no apparent military rationale beyond terror: Plan M's only purpose was to kill. The rebels broke into flats and shot the occupants; one young girl was shot in the neck as she looked out of a hospital window; Securitate men also broke into hospitals and shot patients and staff. There were terrorists on the seventh floor of the Intercontinental Hotel that Friday night shooting down into the streets while the few journalists who had arrived by then were on other floors. There was constant shooting inside the main railway station. It was not simply a matter of staying out of the range of cross-fire between the Army and the rebels: everybody was a potential target, every street a death trap. The walk from the British embassy to the Intercontinental Hotel is not far and usually takes only 15 minutes. That Friday, it took one and a half hours, much of the time spent crouching in doorways, beneath cars, and next to bleeding victims. The bodies laid out each day in the make-shift morgues all tended to have just one or two bullet holes in them, an indication of the skill of the rebels and proof, perhaps, of the belief that their sophisticated weaponry included night and laser

The fighting in Bucharest was bitter, and random, as Securitate 'bandits' appeared all over the city. (Photo: Dod Miller)

sights. Similar scenes, similar murders, were taking place in cities all over the country.

The television station became the temporary seat of the new Government of Romania. Journalists appeared on screen and apologised for having lied to the people in the past, declaring that henceforth they would only publish or broadcast the truth. The self-appointed Government issued instructions and broadcast appeals and news. It asked for people to set up vigilante groups to stop and search every car for concealed weapons. It announced that the dictator's son, Nicu, had been arrested trying to get to the airport with a woman friend. More important, it was able to announce that Nicolai and Elena Ceausescu had been captured. They had landed the helicopter at one of their residences, loaded it with suitcases and then taken off again for a military airport to take flight, their presumed destination China. On the way, Nicolai had panicked, fearful of the loyalty of the troops at the airfield, and instead the helicopter had landed in a field and a local van and driver had been hijacked before they were ignominiously captured. But no proof of this capture was provided, so it did not dampen the desperation of the rebels.

The fighting continued for four days. Rebels who were captured showed no remorse and said only that they were sorry they had not been able to kill more people. At times the revolution came close to defeat, with the provisional Government appealing to foreign governments for ammunition as well as aid. Christmas Day was a bloody

A man runs to take food for soldiers as the people of Bucharest casually watch their own revolution. (Photo: Dod Miller)

affair; there was no peace on earth and certainly no goodwill to all men. But people went to church; and the Church began nervously to explain exactly why it had been so obsequious and obedient to the dictatorship for so many years. After the Timisoara massacre, the Patriarch had still found time and reason to send Ceausescu a letter of congratulations for another year of benign rule.

The turning point came when the Ceausescus, Nicolai and Elena, were put on trial. By any normal standards it was not a fair trial. Justice was summary, execution quick. There was muted criticism from Western governments, who felt that a new government devoted to democracy and the rule of law ought to have started as it meant to go on. Some Romanians agreed that the Ceausescus had been killed too quickly, but for a different reason: they would liked to have seen them killed slowly – very slowly. But it was not a judicial decision to hold the trial, it was a military necessity. The Securitate rebels were gaining the upper hand, and were even attacking the barracks where the Ceausescus were being held. When the decision to execute the presidential couple was taken, the loyalists were gaining ground and were close to freeing the Ceausescus from an outgunned and undertrained provincial Army garrison. Sylviu Brucan, a Salvation Front member said later that 'if Nicolai Ceausescu could have taken command of state security troops, Romania would have become a blood bath with hundreds of thousands of dead'.

The trial was a bizarre mixture of Kafka and Alice in Wonderland, ranging widely from charges of genocide to the grandiose titles the couple had awarded themselves.

NICOLAI CEAUSESCU: I only recognise the Grand National Assembly. I will only speak in front of it.

PROSECUTOR: In the same way he refused to hold a dialogue with the people, now he also refuses to speak with us. He always claimed to act and speak on behalf of the people, to be a beloved son of the people, but he only tyrannised the people all the time. You are faced with charges that you held really sumptuous celebrations on all holidays at your house. The details are known. These two defendants procured the most luxurious foodstuffs and clothes from abroad. They were even worse than the king, the former King of Romania. The people only received 200 grams per day, against an identity card. These two defendants have robbed the people, and not even today do they want to talk. They are cowards. We have data concerning both of them. I ask the Chairman of the Prosecutor's Office to read the bill of indictment.

CHIEF PROSECUTOR: Esteemed Chairman of the Court, today we have to pass a verdict on the defendants Nicolai Ceausescu and Elena Ceausescu who have committed the following offences: Crimes against the people. They carried out acts that are incompatible with human dignity and social thinking; they acted in a despotic and criminal way; they destroyed the people whose leaders they claimed to be. Because of the crimes they committed against the people, I plead, on behalf of the victims of these two tyrants, for the death sentence for the two defendants. The bill of indictment contains the following points: Genocide, in accordance with Article 356 of the Penal Code. Two: Armed attack on the people and the state power, in accordance with Article 163 of the Penal Code. The destruction of buildings and state institutions, undermining of the national economy, in accordance with Articles 165 and 145 of the Penal Code. They obstructed the normal process of the economy.

PROSECUTOR: Did you hear the charges? Have you understood them?

CEAUSESCU: I do not answer, I will only answer questions before the Grand National Assembly. I do not recognize this court. The charges are incorrect, and I will not answer a single question here.

PROSECUTOR [to Elena]: You have always been wiser and more ready to talk, a scientist. You were the most important aide, the number two in the cabinet, in the Government. Did you know about the genocide in Timisoara?

ELENA CEAUSESCU: What genocide? By the way, I will not answer any more questions.

PROSECUTOR: Did you know about the genocide or did you, as a chemist, only deal with polymers? You, as a scientist, did you know about it? [At this point Nicolai Ceausescu steps in and defends her.]

CEAUSESCU: Her scientific papers were published abroad!

PROSECUTOR: And who wrote the papers for you, Elena?

ELENA CEAUSESCU: Such impudence! I am a member and the chairwoman of the Academy of Sciences. You cannot talk to me in such a way!

PROSECUTOR: That is to say, as a Deputy Prime Minister you did not know about the genocide?

CEAUSESCU: She was not a Deputy Prime Minister, but the First Deputy Prime Minister!

The military trial continued in this strange and unjudicial fashion until the sentence was read: the Ceausescus were sentenced to death, to be carried out immediately. Every soldier present volunteered to be part of the firing squad. 'I was like a mother to you all', said a still uncomprehending Elena. The official video of the execution shows only the face of the dead Nicolai; as the three man execution squad performed their task they all lost control and emptied their magazines into the couple whose last wish had been to die together.

On Tuesday, the day after Christmas, the video was shown on Romanian television, followed by the Ode to Joy from Beethoven's Ninth Symphony. The dead face of Nicolai Ceausescu held in a

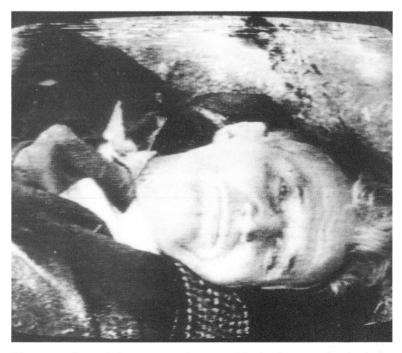

The picture that ended resistance in Romania: Nicolai Ceausescu lies dead, shot by a firing squad on Christmas Day. (Photo: Dod Miller)

dramatic freeze-frame, took the will out of many rebels and the fighting began to die down. There could be no further political reason to carry on fighting, only personal survival and deep-grained hostility. Sporadic sounds of gunfire could still be heard throughout the country, but it gradually diminished. An uneasy peace was settling as the first winter snow began to fall on the living and the dead. In Ceausescu's birthplace, villagers danced on his parents' grave.

Settling too, was an unreal silence. For the first few days of peace, people were treated to pictures of the apartments and houses where their rulers had lived. To them, the houses were of unbelievable grandeur and opulence, the cupboards full of unimaginable luxuries. To Westerners, used to dictators like Ferdinand Marcos, the homes of the Ceausescus were surprisingly mundane, almost disappointing. Tours were organised of the huge palace that had been built in the centre of Bucharest, with its more than 1000 rooms. Tours were also arranged of hospitals and factories where one could see the deprivations and the squalor forced on his beloved working class by Nicolai Ceausescu. When it had been dangerous to parade in the streets of Romania, people had taken the risk and paraded. Now that it was safe to do so, the streets were empty save for small groups tending the memorials to the dead. There were no meetings, and there seemed to be no public discussion of what the future might hold. People had had a common enemy, but not a common purpose. If freedom was a drug, then a lot of people seemed to be enduring cold turkey: the first free New Year's Day in living memory, the start of a new decade and a new era for the country passed by with numbing quietness. People were busy grieving for the dead, or still queueing for food. The provisional Government had unwisely thrown open warehouses of food without any attempt at rationing, with the result that people had stockpiled and there were once again acute shortages.

Perhaps they were daunted by the huge task facing them of reforming the country, a task so enormous it almost makes the fighting look the easy part. Under popular pressure to increase living standards immediately, the National Salvation Front abandoned the austerity programme decreed by Ceausescu. Consumption of electricity has increased by 40 percent since the revolution. Imports from Soviet bloc countries in the spring of 1990 were three times as high as during the same period in 1989. Romania is expected to spend $125 million on Western consumer goods in the first quarter of 1990, compared to practically nothing a year ago. Putting a little more in the shops has proved relatively easy. But any new government is likely to have much more difficulty in getting rid of the central planning system. Western economists estimate that more than 25 percent of the labour force could lose their jobs if unprofitable industries are closed down. The industrial infrastructure is considered several decades out of date. It is the classic dilemma of all East European countries as they attempt to dismantle four decades of Communism, compounded in this case by the fact that centralised controls were much stronger in Romania than elsewhere. Vigorous economic reform would almost certainly lead to a further short term drop in living standards as subsidies are removed, but postponement could exacerbate the crisis.

The suddenness of the revolution was underlined by the political unpreparedness. Romania's writers and intellectuals held a press conference to outline their plans for the future of the country, and it soon became embarrassingly evident that they didn't have any. The pre-war Peasants' Party was hurriedly reformed. Ex-King Michael let the country know that he would be prepared to return, but got little response. More parties sprang up. While all this was going on, the National Salvation Front was consolidating its position. An *ad hoc* group that had held the country together during the revolution, it had earlier declared that it would dissolve itself after the elections had been held. Now it showed a desire to become a party, to fight the election itself.

It had organised the country's provisional Government along lines that were all too familiar to the Romanian public – Communist Party lines. There was a Government, with ministers, but the real power lay in an Executive Council, a Politburo by another name. The Prime Minister was not a member of the Politburo. Many of the leaders of the Front were former Communists, who had held high office under Ceausescu before falling from grace. At the provincial level, it also includes many Army generals and bureaucrats who simply switched sides when it became clear that the dictatorship was crumbling. In most traditional revolutions – the French and Russian revolutions, for example – one political class is replaced by another. The Romanian revolution has been more of a liberation than a revolution. The same class of people has remained in power, even if it claims to think and act differently now that the dictator has gone. The National Salvation Front has become known as the Personal Salvation Front, and not just by its enemies.

The Soviet Union was one of the first countries to recognise the new National Salvation Front as the legitimate Government of Romania. In a message to President Ion Iliescu, Soviet President Mikhail Gorbachov praised the Romanian people's struggle for freedom and democracy against the forces of totalitarianism. Iliescu, a former classmate of Gorbachov at Moscow State University, appears to be highly regarded by the Kremlin as a reform-minded Communist in the Soviet leader's mould.

The experience of Communism under Ceausescu, however, has left most Romanians with a total mistrust of any political philosophy that could be described as socialist. Posters and propaganda signs extolling the Communist Party have been ripped off factories and apartment blocks across the country. The Communist symbol has been torn out of the Romanian flag and the Party itself – which once claimed the loyalty of 2.8 million Romanians – has virtually ceased to exist as an effective political organisation, admitting that it allowed itself to be swamped and drowned under Ceausescu's policies and personality. 'We openly admit that in the dark dictatorship period, the Party compromised itself before the people and before history', a humble statement said.

The Museum of Art took the brunt of the fighting and was left in ruins. (Photo: Dod Miller)

But it isn't enough. The Romanian people now have no time for seemingly abstract discussions about the difference between Ceausescu's Communism and benevolent Communism. They are suspicious and resentful of Iliescu, a Communist who was dismissed from a Party post by Ceausescu in 1971 because he was considered a potential rival for the leadership, but remained on the Party's Central Committee until 1984. Sylviu Brucan, an influential member of the Executive Council, was a trusted ambassador to Washington and the United Nations. Brucan was forced to give up some of his posts after an ill-judged interview to the Western press in which he said, basically, that only one and a half million Romanians were intelligent and the rest had to be led like children. Many of the Army commanders appointed by Ceausescu are still in place.

In the post-revolution days, Romanians have turned cheerfully to the pleasures of character assassination. Deprived of a political dictionary for so long, they are learning a violent language. There are now frequent and regular demonstrations throughout the country, calling for the removal of former Party officials from senior posts both in the Government and in local affairs. The people of Timisoara voted the National Salvation Front out of local power. Very few key people from the Ceausescu era have been arrested, and even fewer brought to trial. A show trial of the four most hated men in the country resulted in life imprisonment for all of them, and trials of Ceausescu's brother and children are planned (Nicu is charged with ordering Securitate to fire on demonstrators in Sibiu). But there is a suspicion that a lot of senior people will not stand trial because they might reveal too much in court about the activities of their colleagues, now jostling for power. There is even a suspicion that this fear might have helped precipitate the rapid execution of the Ceausescus.

The anger and the impatience have fuelled old hostilities and created new ones. Television is once again distrusted as it declines to give equal time to all political parties and remains in the hands of the Front, now a fully constituted political party. The Front has been obliged to create an interim Parliament to accommodate all political parties, but it has managed at the same time to appoint the Government ministers and so effectively retain control of the Parliament.

Romania has ended its long dark night of suffering with a few bright days of violence and death. It appears unlikely that the May elections will bring an end to this pain.

Building a new continent

The revolutions that swept across Eastern Europe were swift and simple. The populations shrugged off Communism as if it were an old garment, and left it lying in the gutter. Only in Romania was there bloodshed: elsewhere, governments that had looked secure, if unloved, turned out to be about as stable as a house of cards.

All that had preserved them against the verdict of the people was the belief that if Communist power were threatened anywhere in Eastern Europe, Soviet force would restore it. It was the gradual dissolution of this belief, gathering pace throughout 1989, which made peaceful revolutions possible. There remained, of course, the risk that the regimes would defend themselves with guns, even if they could no longer depend on support from outside. But only in Romania did this happen.

Why did the governments not fight harder? In China, after all, the rule of the Party was defended in June 1989 by brute force, and Communists have in the past shown little hesitation in using every instrument of the state in their own interests. One reason is that Eastern Europe managed to avoid what the Polish Solidarity activist Adam Michnik calls the Kabul Syndrome.

'In Kabul, the people in government know that only the guillotine awaits them if they cede any power', Michnik told the *International Herald Tribune* in an interview in February. The situation in Poland was different; Michnik, now a member of Parliament and editor-in-chief of a newspaper, had just eaten breakfast at an international conference in Davos with General Jaruzelski, the man who put him in jail for six years.

'Having breakfast with the man who made me a prisoner is part of a logic that I admit is not the logic of justice', Michnik said. 'But the logic of justice is the logic of civil war in the case of Poland today. If we do not reach compromise with the people who led the old system, if we do not adapt them into the transformation we are making, we would have to fight them.'

So the Party ceded power in exchange for an implicit agreement that its members would not face trial, imprisonment or execution for their past crimes – a peaceful evolution that was not inevitable, but followed a pattern first established in Poland, and then in Hungary.

The ruling parties did not go willingly, but only when their own failures could no longer be covered up or explained away. They crashed, like an airliner running out of fuel, when they finally exhausted their reserves of political legitimacy.

None of the ruling parties in Eastern Europe had ever enjoyed legitimacy in the Western sense of offering themselves to the electorate and winning approval in free and fair elections. Their claim was that the Party ruled, in the words of George Schopflin of the London School of Economics, 'because it was the legatee of a Communist revolution, that it was the repository of history, that it was the most rational and efficient force in the state, that it represented the best and most progressive elements of the national tradition'.

Every one of these claims was false. Communism was imposed on Eastern Europe from outside, not generated internally; it did not express national sentiments, but often tried to suppress them; its failure to produce economic success invalidated its claim to efficiency, and its repression of dissent made a mockery of its claims to be progressive. In Eastern Europe, Communism lacked even the twin pillars upon which the legitimacy of the Soviet Party is founded: the claim to have modernised Russia and turned it into a superpower, and the victory over Hitler.

None of the people's revolutions was imposed from outside, even though the Soviet reforms of Mikhail Gorbachov played a part in each of them. They were national revolutions in which populations long enslaved sought to recover their own history. That gives them a far greater chance of succeeding than the regimes they replaced. But there remain the problems which were either created by Communist rule, or were suppressed by it and are now re-emerging: economic failure, political inexperience and nationalist rivalries.

Moscow's imposition of Communism on the region created the illusion of an East European identity. Now free, the populations are able to say things previously forbidden to them: that they have little in common and that they have never even liked each other much. 'It's natural that the Eastern Europeans should love each other now because we're all pleased to see the end of Communism', says Laszlo Lang of the Institute of International Affairs in Budapest. 'It is also evident that in the first stage of change there may be parallels in our politics. But then national developments will take their natural course and we may cease to love each other so much.'

For the moment, though, it is the economic problems that are uppermost. Centrally planned socialism may have eliminated destitution, but it proved unable to produce prosperity. Its failure was camouflaged for many years because it lived off capital accumulated in the earlier period, and excess labour from the countryside; later, money borrowed from the West was used to prop up living standards. Imre Pozgay, the most reform-minded of the Hungarian Communists (now Socialists), reckons that only 10 percent of Hungary's $21 billion debt went on productive purposes: 'The rest was spent on the maintenance of social peace'. In other words, it was eaten. Poland used foreign loans to invest in heavy industry at the wrong time, with disastrous results.

Even East Germany, long believed to be the most successful of the socialist economies, could not satisfy a people daily exposed to West German television. Idealists in East Germany – and a surprising number have remained uncorrupted by 40 years of Communism – had hoped that a middle course might exist between the rigidities of central planning and the free market of the West, but the people have made it plain that they have little appetite for it.'Most of the ordinary people', said an East German churchwoman, 'actually have only one alternative in view, and that is Western-style Neckermann democracy' (Neckermann is a West German mail order house).

The difficulties Eastern Europe faces are not unique. Western Europe has found an answer to very similar problems within the European Community. Not only has the EC provided a successful economic framework, and made wars between its members unthinkable, but it has also helped sustain young democracies in Spain and Portugal. It is hardly surprising that it has acted like a magnet to the Eastern and Central Europeans, with its promises of everything that their own economic organisation, Comecon, has failed to deliver.

The common aspiration is to join the EC, or at least to devise a way of sharing in its prosperity. In an address to the Polish Parliament at the end of January, the playwright Vaclav Havel – who began 1989 in jail and ended it as President of Czechoslovakia – urged Poland, Hungary and possibly other Eastern European countries to join Czechoslovakia in a coordinated bid to return to Europe after the years of Soviet domination.

'Before us is a historic opportunity to fill a large political vacuum created in Central Europe after the fall of the Habsburgs ... we should not compete over who is going to overtake whom and who will first win a seat in some European body, but we should do just the opposite: help each other in the spirit of that solidarity with which in worse times you protested against our repression and we against yours.'

Relations between the Community and Eastern Europe were already warming up before the revolutions of 1989. The possibility of diplomatic relations between the EC and Comecon was envisaged in a joint declaration in June 1988, and in August and September of the same year, diplomatic relations were established with the GDR,

Bulgaria, Hungary and Poland. But the pace accelerated in July 1989, when the Economic Summit in Paris called on the European Commission to organise a programme of economic cooperation and support for Eastern Europe.

This was a remarkable and unexpected initiative, elevating the Commission to a central role at a key moment. It came about as a result of a suggestion made by Commission President Jacques Delors at the dinner held for heads of government on 14 July, and was included in the declaration on East–West relations issued the following morning as a result of an amendment proposed by the West German Chancellor Helmut Kohl. For Kohl, it provided an international framework for West German efforts, easing problems that were then emerging in his coalition. For President Bush, whose own plan for an international consortium had met some opposition, it was a natural alternative. The fact that the Commission has no mandate to negotiate on behalf of countries that are not members of the Community was overlooked. The programme was launched at a meeting in Brussels on 1 August 1989 of senior officials from 24 nations that became known as the Group of 24, or G24. They were the 12 European Community nations, the six nations of the European Free Trade Area (Austria, Switzerland, Finland, Iceland, Norway and Sweden), the US, Canada, Japan, Turkey, New Zealand and Australia. Together, they represent the vast majority of the world's economic muscle. At the August meeting, and subsequent meetings in September, November and December, G24 entrusted the European Commission with the task of creating a plan of assistance for the restructuring of the Eastern European economies. One day this may be seen as a turning point in history, the moment when Western Europe reached out to embrace the other half of Europe, so long separated from it by artificial barriers.

At the start, only Poland and Hungary had begun the reform process. A plan, called PHARE (Poland and Hungary: Assistance for Economic Restructuring) was drawn up, with five main sectors for concerted action. They were the restructuring of Polish agriculture; improved access of Polish and Hungarian goods to Western markets; the promotion of investment in Poland and Hungary; vocational training (executives, managers, teachers, and students); and the improvement of the environment.

By the middle of November, when Delors visited Warsaw and Budapest, promises of financial support for these five sectors amounted to almost 1 billion ECU ($1.2 billion) for Poland, and half as much for Hungary. After his visit, Delors reported directly to an emergency summit of Community heads of government in Paris on 18 November. He warned them that Poland, in particular, was in a desperate economic plight and could face a crisis without food aid to see it through the winter.

As the other dominoes fell in Eastern Europe, the PHARE programme was extended. In January, the EC Commissioner for External Affairs, Dutchman Frans Andriessen, made a barnstorming tour through Czechoslovakia, Romania and Bulgaria. He talked to the new government leaders about future relations with the Community and listened to their appeals for long term financial aid. Community foreign ministers met early in February and agreed to extend the programme to five more countries: Bulgaria, East Germany, Czechoslovakia, Romania and Yugoslavia. In return, they made it clear that the Eastern Europeans would have to guarantee the rule of law, the upholding of human rights, a multi-party system, free and fair elections, and economic liberalisation leading to the establishment of market economies.

At the same time, rapid progress was being made towards the establishment of a new bank, the European Bank for Reconstruction and Development, whose main function was to be to provide funds for the restoration of market economies in Eastern Europe. This idea originated with President Mitterrand of France, who intended to put it forward at the December meeting of the Community heads of government in Strasbourg as a French initiative. Delors went to see him and argued strongly that the idea would have a much better chance of success if it was presented as a Community initiative. Since Mitterrand was at the time in the chair of the Community, he agreed to this change of plan, and despite some initial British reluctance all 12 concurred.

The creation of the bank was agreed at a meeting in Paris held on 15–16 January and attended by 34 countries. No final decisions were taken at this meeting, but the broad outlines emerged. The total capital of the bank will be 10 billion ECUs ($12 billion), half of it subscribed by the Community members. The US, Japan, the European Free Trade Area and the Soviet Union are each expected to take 8.5 percent, and the other members of Comecon about 6.5 percent. It will lend money to private businesses in Eastern Europe and, despite Mrs Thatcher's doubts, to state-owned industry as well.

In opening the conference, Mitterrand urged haste. 'It is right to take one's time, but sometimes one takes too much and events move faster than decisions and, in this instance, this is the risk we would run if we didn't act quickly', he told the delegates. They responded to his urging, and the bank was expected to be established by Easter 1990. The Czech delegate at the meeting even offered it a home, an elegant building in Prague of which he said: 'It used to be a bank, but for the past 40 years it's been a museum of Marxist-Leninism, and we don't need it any more'. There was laughter, in which the Soviet delegate joined. The chances are, however, that the Community countries will insist on a base for the bank within the EC – there is no shortage of volunteers, including London.

Mrs Thatcher initially doubted the usefulness of the bank because she believes that loans are not necessarily the best way to help economies already drowning in debt. It is a view shared by many bankers, who say that Poland has already gone beyond the ability to service its debt, while Bulgaria and Hungary have reached the absolute limit of what they can afford to borrow. Czechoslovakia is less heavily borrowed, while Romania is unique in having no foreign debt at all, President Ceausescu having paid it off during the 1980s by squeezing his people dry and selling abroad the fuel and food they needed to live on.

Since 1981 the Polish debt has been rescheduled five times, but Poland is none the less in arrears to its creditors. Like many Latin American countries, the point has been passed when rescheduling is sufficient to make the burden of debt sustainable. At $41 billion, the Polish debt is far and away the largest of the Eastern bloc. In spite of this, Poland is to receive another $170 million from the International Monetary Fund, in addition to the $1 billion pledged by Western governments as a fund for stabilising the zloty. The IMF's prescriptions for repairing the crippled Polish economy suggest exactly the kind of price rises and removals of subsidy which have caused riots elsewhere in the world.

Eugenio Lari, Director of the World Bank's European operations, warns that 'Poland cannot regain its balance and service its existing debt'. The only way for the heavily indebted Eastern countries to finance the transition to market-based economies is for Western governments and banks to share the burden by forgiving some of the existing debt. Nevertheless, the Bank is prepared to advance as much as $7.5 billion over the next three years for the four Eastern European countries that are now members of the bank – Poland, Hungary, Romania and Yugoslavia. The other three – Czechoslovakia, Bulgaria and East Germany – have all shown an interest in joining, and they too will no doubt qualify for loans when they do.

The difficulty is that the economies crippled by Communism cannot evolve into market economies without help – but that help runs the risk of worsening their plight, with inflation raging, real wages low, and capital fleeing abroad. They could, in short, evolve as easily into Latin American economies as into Western European ones. In 1945, Britain was lent $2 billion by the US, the equivalent of $20 billion today. In two years it was all gone. It took Britain seven years to abolish food rationing after the end of the Second World War, and even then, in 1952, the economy was considered too weak to sustain full-scale currency convertibility. Indeed, exchange controls were not finally removed until 1979. The evolution into free market economies did not prove an easy matter for Western Europe, however inevitable it may appear in retrospect. There is no reason to suppose it will be any easier for the East.

One danger seen by economists is that parts of Eastern Europe will become a source of cheap labour, used for simple assembly plants for goods to be sold in the West. While this will provide jobs, it is not a rapid route to economic development, as many developing countries can attest. The East Germans face this danger in acute form. A second danger is that the hunger for Western-style consumer goods will suck out the hard currency earnings, slowing the pace of investment in productive machinery. Free trade may be desirable, but it may not necessarily be the first thing to be desired. The liberation of trade within the Eastern bloc, together with some trade barriers against imports from the West, may be a more hopeful route. As Professor Susan Strange of the European University Institute in Florence has pointed out, this was one of the strategies of the Marshall Plan which put Western Europe on the road to economic success in the late 1940s. The US used the leverage of Marshall Aid to make Europeans liberalise trade between themselves, but they allowed them to use exchange controls to discriminate against American imports. Without such controls, Professor Strange says, Europe would quickly have run out of dollars buying attractive and competitively priced American goods.

The single element agreed by almost all economists is the need for debt relief, particularly for Poland, Hungary and Bulgaria. 'The next generation in Poland must know that it is not expected to pay for the sins of 40 years of Communist rule', says Professor Jeffrey Sachs of Harvard, who has advised Solidarity and the Coalition Government in Poland. 'At a crucial moment in its history Germany did not get debt relief, and that contributed to Hitler's rise. After World War II, Germany did get relief, and that led to an economic miracle.'

The collapse of authority in Eastern Europe has left its countries adrift. The governments that took over (with the exception of the coalition in Poland) have no permanence; their mandate is simply to guide the way to free elections and then to leave the floor to proper governments. Internationally, the picture is equally fluid. The economic and military alliances that determined the foreign policy of Eastern Europe, Comecon and the Warsaw Pact, are in a state of dissolution. 'History is at a turning point, just as it was in 1848, 1918 and 1945', says Professor Michael Sturmer of West Germany's Research Institute for International Politics and Security.

The barriers that divided Europe for two generations have been broken, but nobody is yet sure of the long term implications of this change. No longer do Russians and Americans have to offer any Grand Design, but without it Europe is rather like a man who has opened his mouth to speak, but doesn't know what to say. What will replace the system of blocs that has kept the peace so successfully by raising the risks of war so high? Will the European Community grow until it encompasses the whole of Europe, East, West, and Central? And what is to be the future of the North Atlantic Treaty Organisation, a military alliance of free nations that has seen its aims realised in the East but must now come to terms with the diminishing Soviet threat?

The history of Eastern and Central Europe is a pattern of empires rather than nation states. The Ottoman, the Habsburg and the Russian empires have in turn controlled large parts of the region. It has never been stable for long; the 40-year freeze brought about by Soviet control after 1945 is the exception rather than the rule. Both world wars, and the Cold War, began in Eastern Europe. Unlike Western Europe, where nation and state are usually coterminous, the nations of Eastern Europe do not fit neatly within the boundaries of their own states. Only Poland, where 95 percent of the population is Polish and Roman Catholic, and Hungary, where 90 percent is Magyar, are ethnically homogeneous. Czechoslovakia is a federation of Czechs and Slovaks, while Yugoslavia contains six distinct nationalities. There are significant minorities in both Romania (ethnic Hungarians) and in Bulgaria (Turks).

All this means that there is no reassuring past into which Eastern Europe can now slip back, no ancient formulas for peace and prosperity that can be dug out and dusted off. The Soviet Union, shorn of its Eastern Europe shield, will remain the dominant military power in Europe, a powerful neighbour and a difficult one to live with. But the single most powerful economic power will be a reunited Germany. As the Soviet Union begins to fall apart, Germany is coming together, in one of those great shifts that occur only once in a lifetime. Building a secure framework within which such changes can take place peacefully is a tremendous challenge.

In Western Europe, economic, political and security issues have traditionally been the responsibility of different organisations. The European Community and the European Free Trade Area have an economic mandate. The security of Western Europe has been the responsibility of Nato, an organisation that has proved much more than simply a military alliance. Both the EC and Nato have contributed to political harmonisation, with a common foreign policy beginning to emerge through the political cooperation machinery of the EC, and a coherent security strategy established through discussions in Nato.

The evolution of these two organisations, with their overlapping membership, has helped create a Western Europe strong both economically and militarily. But they have done more than that. They have eliminated the possibility of disputes between their members leading to war, a considerable achievement which is often overlooked only because it is taken for granted. Through the EC and Nato, West Germany has emerged as a model international citizen, a good neighbour and a sound ally. Potentially dangerous conflicts, like that between Turkey and Greece, have been managed without war. It is hard to be certain that all this would have been achieved without both these organisations.

In the East, potential disagreements between neighbours have been suppressed beneath a doctrine of internationalism imposed by the Soviet Union. It did not solve the problems of the area, but conealed them. Beneath this suffocating blanket, regional disputes have survived and may now be ready to emerge once more. The long series of traumatic events in Eastern Europe – the collapse of the Ottoman and Austro-Hungarian empires, the Versailles Agreements of 1919 that redrew the map of Europe, the Nazi-Soviet Pact of 1939 and the Yalta Agreement of 1945 – have all displaced peoples and frontiers, creating potential flashpoints. There are at least six potential frontier disputes, and more than a dozen pockets of displaced ethnic groups throughout Eastern Europe that could cause trouble.

By far the greatest danger (outside the Soviet Union itself, which is another story) is in Yugoslavia, a country that did not have a revolution during 1989 but is often included among those that did because it has a broadly reformist administration. Yugoslavia consists of six nations, uneasily co-existing in a society that appears to have proved that reform Communism does not work. Economic failure has intensified disagreements between the politically dominant Serbs, who represent nine million of the country's 24 million people, and the more developed but less numerous Croats and Slovenes, and the nationalistic Albanians in the province of Kosovo. The tensions in Yugoslavia are now close to breaking point, and demonstrate the dangers that will face other Eastern European countries if their escape from the Communist straightjacket does not bring economic prosperity.

In Czechoslovakia, potential conflicts exist between the majority Czechs and the minority Slovaks, who are less prosperous and resent it. There is also a minority of ethnic Hungarians living among the Slovaks. In Bulgaria, relations between the Bulgars and the Turkish minority, who represent 8.5 percent of the population, are already bad. One of the first fruits of the liberalisation in Bulgaria was a massive demonstration against the Turks, which does not suggest that greater freedom will produce greater tolerance.

As for Hungary and Romania, not even Solomon would dare

adjudicate in their long-standing disagreements over Transylvania, acquired by Romania 70 years ago. For many Hungarians, the loss of Transylvania is a wound that still bleeds, while Romanians, who were already a majority in Transylvania when the transfer took place, consider the time of Hungarian rule to have been one of oppression. This old sore was made worse by the policies of the Romanian dictator Nicolai Ceausescu, who systematically deprived the 2.6 million ethnic Hungarians of their rights. While everybody suffered under Ceausescu, Hungarians suffered most. The Government in Budapest, obedient to the rule that national squabbles should not exist under Communism and should therefore not be admitted, did not make the mistreatment of ethnic Hungarians in Romania an issue until 1985.

Romania- towns and national minorities

With the removal of Ceausescu, the Hungarian minority is reasserting itself, with plans to establish a Hungarian-language university. If there are any attempts to suppress such expressions of national identity, there will be serious trouble. Budapest fears that there will be a flood of refugees over the border, into a country that is already having difficulty providing for its own people.

Romania itself has claims over part of Moldavia, now in the Soviet Union, and potential claims against Bulgaria over the Black Sea region of Dobruja. Poland, for understandable historical reasons, is obsessed by its western border with East Germany, created at Yalta, when the victorious powers shifted Poland physically westward, taking territory from Germany to replace that which Stalin insisted on taking from eastern Poland.

The problems, then, are of two kinds. Substantial national minorities within most East European countries threaten to make progress towards democracy more difficult, and the frontiers between countries are drawn in the wrong places, as many Eastern Europeans would see it. This threatens a future of internal dissent and international dispute, if the right decisions are not taken in the next 10 years.

Most analysts expect instability to be a continuing feature in Eastern Europe for some considerable time. Even if all goes well, new structures will emerge only slowly, and not all the tensions described above will be skilfully handled. In the background there is likely to be continuing trouble in the Soviet Union, whose nationality problems are even worse than those of Eastern Europe. The task thus becomes one of devising an international framework durable enough to deal with great instability. The idea that now Communism has retreated we can all live together in peace and harmony is not one that is shared by many experienced observers.

It may not, however, be necessary to invent any new institutions. Europe is already abundantly supplied with them. First there are the two military alliances, although the Warsaw Pact is likely to fade into insignificance. In addition Western Europe is linked by another military alliance, the Western European Union (WEU), which brings together nine nations. (It is as part of the treaty setting up WEU that British forces are based in West Germany.) Although WEU has been overshadowed by Nato for many years, it may have a more significant role in future. For economic and political harmonisation there are the EC and EFTA. On cultural and legal matters there is the Council of Europe, an inter-governmental organisation based in Strasbourg. And, finally, there is the structure created by the 35-nation Conference on Security and Cooperation in Europe, which incorporates the whole of Europe (less Albania), the Soviet Union, the US and Canada. The CSCE began in Helsinki in 1975, which is why its deliberations are sometimes referred to as 'the Helsinki Process'. Intended as a point of contact between the two blocs, its agreements cover human rights, economic cooperation, and confidence-building measures in the military field.

What shape will the new Europe take? One major change appears certain – the reunification of Germany. Much will hang on the precise way it is carried out. We shall return to the question later, but will examine first a number of possible outcomes to the debate now raging over future political and security arrangements in the continent.

There are at least four possible scenarios. The worst, and the least likely, is a return to rampant nationalism in Europe, with the balance of power being held by the strong. Reform has failed in Eastern Europe, the drive towards Western European integration has faltered, the alliances have disappeared, and the US has reverted to isolationism. It would be the worst of all worlds, and the chances of it happening are very small. We have been this way before, in the period between the two great wars, and we are unlikely to make exactly the same mistakes again.

The much more likely outcome, at least in the short term, is a continuation of the status quo. The existing structure of alliances will survive – at least on the Western side – and American forces will remain in Europe. The Warsaw Pact will cease to have much significance, but the threat from the Soviet Union will remain, and will keep Nato alive. A reunited Germany will remain in Nato. The EC will continue to flourish but will not extend its capacities far, being too involved in encouraging economic development in the East. This is broadly the future that Mrs Thatcher envisages.

Enthusiasts for European unity have yet another view. The EC has become the dominant force, perhaps taking on the security role of Nato by merging with the WEU. The nations of Eastern Europe have become closely associated with the EC, either as full members or as an 'outer circle' enjoying most of the economic advantages of membership without loss of national sovereignty. The six EFTA nations occupy a similar position. The EC's influence stretches from Brest to Brest-Litovsk. It forms an inner circle, a United States of Europe, surrounded by two concentric circles made up of EFTA and the Eastern Europeans. Some US forces remain in Europe, but only in token numbers.

The fourth possible scenario is yet more visionary. It sees the CSCE as the framework for a new common security system for the whole of Europe, including the Soviet Union. The CSCE would develop a permanent secretariat, and be responsible for a series of arms control negotiations aimed at denuclearising Europe and building trust between states. Individual nations would adopt non-provocative defence policies. The two military alliances would merge into a European Security Organisation, responsible for security in a region stretching from Vancouver to Vladivostock. The Common European Home so often spoken of by Mikhail Gorbachov would have been created. This future is the vision of the Soviet Union, and of parties of the left in many nations of Western Europe, including West Germany.

*

The different scenarios sketched above are not mutually exclusive. It might be possible to 'mix and match' elements from one with another. For example, almost everybody assumes a continuing future for the EC and for CSCE; they differ in the importance they attach to each. Some see the alliances fading away, or adopting a more political and less military character. Others see the creation of fresh international organisations, in the Balkans or in Central and Eastern Europe, to meet the special needs of the nations of the region.

Zbigniew Brzezinski, born in Warsaw and an American citizen who served as National Security Adviser to President Carter, believes, for example, that Poland and Czechoslovakia should form a federation to create a buffer between Germany in the West and the Soviet Union in the East. 'The geopolitical situation indicates that there should be cooperation between Slovaks, Czechs and Poles', Brzezinski says. Such a federation was proposed during the Second World War but was scuttled by the Kremlin, as was a similar proposal for a confederation between Romania and Bulgaria. So far, Brzezinski's idea has not been taken up by either Czechoslovakia or Poland.

Gianni De Michelis, the Italian Foreign Minister, is enthusiastic about collaboration in Central Europe. Together with the foreign ministers of Hungary, Austria and Yugoslavia, he took part in a meeting in Budapest in November 1989 which set up a framework of cooperation between the four countries in industrial, scientific, cultural, environmental, transport and telecommunications matters. The quadrangular initiative, as this relationship is called, is not intended to replace existing commitments to alliances or other organisations, or to substitute for more distant ambitions like the expansion of the EC or the creation of a Common European Home. 'Uniting the European Community is a complex process', says De Michelis, 'and, with the possible exception of one or two countries, I cannot see how the 12 can be joined by other partners before the turn of the century . . . for this reason we are actively seeking forms of very close association which stop short of full membership.'

As for the new democracies of Eastern Europe, most have already made it clear that their own wish is to join the existing Western European organisations. Poland, Hungary, East Germany, Yugoslavia and Czechoslovakia have all made overtures to the EC, while Poland and Hungary have already taken the first steps into the Council of Europe. The response by the EC has been to say that with the possible exception of East Germany, it is not possible to envisage the entry of any of them for at least 10 years. East Germany is different because it appears almost certain to be reunited with West Germany long before then, and will therefore have to be accommodated somehow. The Community has already put off applications from Turkey and Austria, which ought properly to be dealt with first.

What the EC is prepared to do is to negotiate association agreements with the Eastern European applicants, covering trade, technical assistance, financial support, joint infrastructure projects, cultural cooperation and political dialogue. In the past, such association agreements have been signed with aspirants to EC membership such as Greece and Turkey, and have included explicit commitments to eventual full membership. In the case of the Eastern Europeans, Commission officials have made it clear that no such commitment will be agreed, but nor will ultimate membership be excluded. Jacques Delors outlined this policy in a meeting with the Polish Prime Minister, Tadeusz Mazowiecki, in Brussels early in February 1990.

Whether this will be enough to satisfy the East is not yet clear. Czechoslovakia has made it clear that it is seeking an agreement to begin full negotiations for entry within five years, a request it may be difficult to turn down. Others seem certain to make similar demands. The EC will be faced with a tricky decision. Is it to open its doors to the aspirants from the East, as its instincts dictate? Or is it to take the view that it can best discharge its responsibility to Europe as a whole by not enlarging too rapidly or too far? The question has yet to be seriously addressed.

Berndt von Staden, a former state secretary in the Bonn Foreign Ministry, takes the cautious view. He warned in the German foreign policy review, *Aussenpolitik*, that favourable prospects should not be impaired or even gambled away by attempting to achieve too much too fast. He quoted with approval a remark made by Talleyrand to his coachman: 'Jean, va doucement, je suis pressé' – 'Drive slowly, John, I'm in a hurry'.

His view is that helping Eastern Europe is the EC's most important European policy task for many years to come, but that it will be able to discharge this task satisfactorily only if it faces the countries concerned as a friend able not only to act generously but also to determine the terms under which assistance stands the best chances of success. 'It is hardly conceivable that a community can cope with such problems within itself, with the statutory participation of those directly affected', he concludes.

In this view, the EC is not a school in which aspirants learn the rules of democracy and a free market, but a postgraduate department open to those who have already mastered them. Anything else would risk diluting what has already been achieved, and would not be in the best interests of those who are seeking help.

The argument is linked to another one. Is it the Community's task in the next decade to become broader, or deeper? Should it extend its membership without changing its nature – as Mrs Thatcher might argue – or should it intensify existing cooperation in moving towards monetary and economic union while delaying the process of enlargement? Some argue that this is a false dichotomy, and that the Community should become both broader and deeper at the same time, but to others that is putting too much strain on an organisation that has only recently emerged from a period of stagnation itself.

While the revolutions were taking place on the streets of Eastern Europe, one thing remained the same. In their barracks on both sides of the Iron Curtain, soldiers from East and West went about their business as if nothing had changed. The Soviet troops in Czechoslovakia, Hungary, Poland and East Germany, which under Brezhnev would have swung into action to suppress revolt, kept their heads down and did nothing. The US, British and other Nato forces in West Germany watched in fascination as the enemy began to disintegrate in front of them.

The forces of the two alliances are the visible manifestation of the Cold War. Its temperature has been measured for the past 40 years by the progress, or lack of it, in negotiations designed to reduce their numbers. There were some periods of warmer weather, like the early 1970s when arms control deals were struck between Leonid Brezhnev and President Richard Nixon, but there were also sharp frosts. The early 1980s, with the trauma over Euromissiles, was the last of these. Today the Cold War appears to be over, and a real war unimaginable. But the forces to fight it remain in place.

As the threat of war has diminished, public pressure to reduce force levels has grown. Unfortunately, arms control negotiations are long-winded affairs even if the will is there, because any agreement reached must be framed in treaty language, and verification procedures worked out to ensure that neither side is cheating. As a result, arms control almost inevitably lags behind public perception of the threat. Sometimes, agreements are reached which the public is no longer willing to accept because the threat has meanwhile grown: SALT-2, never ratified by the US Senate, is an example of this. More often, as today, the public is impatient for quicker movement than the negotiators can provide. As Hans Binnendijk, Director of Studies at the International Institute for Strategic Studies in London, puts it: 'The European revolutions of 1989 have created a new reality, and European arms control will have to adjust or become irrelevant'.

In the 1970s and 1980s, he says, the purpose of arms control from the Western point of view was to reduce the threat posed by the Warsaw Pact's large advantage in conventional and short-range nuclear forces. 'Three months of revolution in the East are helping to accomplish what 15 years of arms control did not. Now the very existence of the Warsaw Pact is in question.'

Three members of the pact, Czechoslovakia, Poland and Hungary, have so far asked the Soviet Union to remove its troops from their territory. Western governments had expected that most or all of these troops would be withdrawn anyway, given a successful outcome to conventional arms control talks going on under the umbrella of the CSCE in Vienna. But the fact that all three governments demanded their withdrawal underlined the disarray in the pact, and focussed attention on the much larger number of Soviet troops in East Germany. The Czechoslovak demand for the withdrawal of Soviet troops by the end of 1990 was inspired by fears that Mikhail Gorbachov would be overthrown in the Soviet Union and replaced by somebody less willing to accept reform. Similar demands from Poland and Hungary followed within a week. The Soviet Union appears quite willing to respond favourably to these requests; its greatest problem, it claims, is finding housing and jobs for the demobilised troops back home.

Nato has not escaped similar pressures. Opinion in West Germany has for several years been running strongly against Nato plans to modernise its short-range nuclear weapons, most of which would be based on West German soil. Most people now believe that these plans cannot be carried out, not least because of their absurdity in the new circumstances. The range of the rockets would allow them to reach no further than the territory of the newly liberated Eastern nations.

Belgium and the Netherlands have added to Nato's worries by indicating that they want to withdraw part of their forces based in West Germany. The Dutch are aiming to save about £700 million in defence spending by 1995, partly by pulling out 750 men from West Germany, while the Belgian Defence Minister, Guy Coeme, told Brussels newspapers that he had instructed the general staff to work out scenarios for withdrawing all 25,000 Belgian troops. The Nato Secretary General, Manfred Woerner, had earlier expressed concern at the tendency in Nato nations to reduce their defence efforts unilaterally, describing it as 'structural disarmament'. Such moves, he said, were 'wrong and dangerous'.

Faced with the loss of political will on both sides, attempts have been made to accelerate the Conventional Forces in Europe (CFE) talks in Vienna. In his State of the Union address on 31 January 1990, President Bush proposed much deeper cuts in US and Soviet forces in central Europe, to a level of 195,000 on each side. The Soviet Union initially showed reluctance to accept this offer, contending that it would leave the US with an advantage, since it stations another 30,000 troops outside the central region, in Britain, Spain and other countries. But at a meeting in Ottawa in the middle of February between foreign ministers of Nato and the Warsaw Pact, Soviet Foreign Minister Eduard Shevardnadze indicated acceptance of the offer. It will represent a dramatic reduction in Soviet force numbers, which are now about 575,000. The US cut, from 330,000, will be less

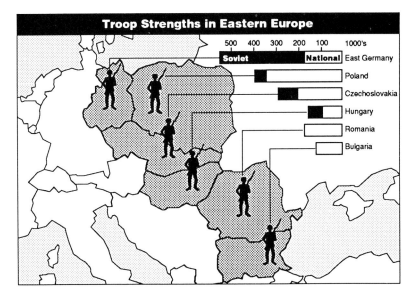

extreme, but the outcome will be what Nato has always sought: a balance of conventional forces in Europe.

Bush's initiative was a recognition that his first offer, of a cut to 275,000, had been overrun by events. It was also designed to cut military spending and help to bring the US deficit under control. He faced little congressional opposition to the plan, which had already been urged on him by influential senators such as Democrat Sam Nunn, Chairman of the Senate Armed Services Committee. The extent to which opinion in the US has shifted was dramatically pointed up by evidence given by Richard Perle, a former assistant secretary of defence, to Mr Nunn's committee.

Perle, once dubbed 'The Prince of Darkness' for his hard line towards the Soviet Union, declared that the political changes in Eastern Europe had eliminated any possibility of a Soviet attack on Western Europe. It was 'simply no longer possible to imagine a cohesive Warsaw Pact, led by Soviet troops, forcing its way through the centre of Europe in a massive invasion', he told the committee on 25 January 1990. 'The canonical threat against which a defensive Nato alliance has long been poised is no longer credible.' Despite his reputation as an archetypal cold warrior, Perle is a shrewd analyst whose views carry weight. If he declared that the Soviet threat of invasion of Western Europe no longer existed, few were prepared to argue.

During 1990, the race will be on to finalise a whole series of arms control agreements, to enable the process to catch up with political developments in Europe. At a superpower summit in Washington in June, Bush and Gorbachov are expected to agree a treaty which will cut their strategic nuclear weapons in half. At a full meeting of the CSCE towards the end of the year, the CFE agreement incorporating the 195,000 limit, and also setting limits for tanks, artillery, armoured vehicles, aircraft and helicopters, is expected to be ready for signature. The US and the Soviet Union also agreed early in February at a series of meetings in Moscow between Secretary of State James Baker and Soviet leaders that both sides would reduce their stocks of chemical weapons, encouraging the hope that the slow-moving talks in Geneva designed to ban such weapons worldwide might now pick up speed.

What these changes represent is a long delayed demobilisation at the end of the Second World War. The West did bring its troops home when Germany was defeated, but was forced to call them up again when Stalin reneged on his promises to allow free elections in Eastern Europe, and the Cold War began. The Soviet Union has never demobilised.

The question that must now be addressed is how far the process is to go. What security system will replace that of the two alliances? The world may have changed, but the old rules of power and the balance of power have not. The Europe of the future will still contain one superpower which may have disavowed any wish for hegemony but which nevertheless will remain stronger than anybody else. Britain and France, once great powers themselves, are sceptical about the prospects for wholesale disarmament and the creation of a continent-wide common security system. Germany, which has abdicated from power politics in the wake of its defeat in the Second World War, regards such a prospect much more favourably, because within such a system it would be able to use its military power not for aggressive purposes, but to increase its political weight. The Royal Navy once played just such a role when Britain was top dog in Europe.

Defenders of the status quo see no reason why the decline of the Warsaw Pact should be mirrored by Nato. To them this is a false symmetry which fails to recognise that the two alliances are different in structure and in purpose. Given the continued existence of the Soviet Union and its preponderance in nuclear and conventional weapons, Nato must in their view survive if Europe is to remain in balance. In particular, the commitment of the US, and the presence of some of its forces on European soil, are unavoidable for the foreseeable future.

Critics are apt to characterise this view as nostalgia for the lost certainties of the Cold War, ridiculing the dependence on nuclear deterrence and the belief that peace can only be maintained by preparing for war. They see a historic opportunity to establish a new security framework slipping by because some Western leaders lack the vision to grasp it. 'We survived the dangers of the Cold War', argues

Professor Ken Booth of the University College of Wales in Aberystwyth in the January 1990 issue of *International Affairs*, 'and the West, on the whole, won it. But what must be won now is the future, and that must be won together ... The challenge of the second post-war era is that of living together, indefinitely, free of the fear of war and with energies freed to deal with all the serious issues the future is set to dump upon us.'

Professor Booth argues for what is known as a 'legitimate international order' or security regime in which all the major powers agree on the permissible aims and limits of foreign policy. International security exists in such a system because none of its members is tempted to challenge the limits, or express dissatisfaction by a revolutionary foreign policy like that pursued by Germany after the Treaty of Versailles. Such an order has existed in Europe before, between the Congress of Vienna in 1815 and the outbreak of the Crimean War in 1853. The Concert of Europe, as it was called, followed the horrors of the Napoleonic Wars and depended on the nations of Europe adopting self-denying ordinances, recognising the values of restraint in international affairs, and communicating effectively despite the differences of ideology between them.

Do the conditions now exist for a new Concert of Europe? Those who are naturally optimistic about the perfectibility of man and who are convinced that the Soviet Union has made a decisive and irreversible change in its foreign policies believe they do. More cynical (or, as they would say, realistic) observers believe that to abandon the traditional rules overnight would amount to negligence or an alarming lack of a sense of history.

In this argument, the role of Germany and the Germans is absolutely central. For 40 years, West Germany has looked both ways: first westward under Konrad Adenauer, who planted his country firmly in Nato and the EC, and then eastward under Willy Brandt and Helmut Schmidt, who remained loyal to Nato but through Ostpolitik also attempted to create an opening into Eastern Europe and the Soviet Union. Helmut Kohl has continued with the same broad policy. Part of the German joy at the developments in Eastern Europe is that it enables them to integrate these two aspects of their foreign policy, at the same time as achieving the unity they have always sought. But where will a united Germany stand on the question of European security policy? That may ultimately determine the whole future of the continent.

When Eastern Europe erupted in the second half of 1989, wise heads declared that the process thus begun might end with the reunification of Germany. But first there would be lengthy discussions involving the Four Powers who retain vestigial responsibilities over the territory of a vanquished foe, meetings of the EC and the CSCE, a

free vote in the East, even – according to Eduard Shevardnadze – an international referendum. Chancellor Kohl was criticised at home by the SPD and the Greens for suggesting that reunification might at last be on the agenda, as if it were somehow presumptuous for the leader of half of a divided country to seek that union with the rest which West Germany's own Basic Law declares to be the nation's objective.

Seldom have minds been changed so fast by events. But it was from the East, not the West, that the main impetus for union came. Ordinary East Germans, with no stake in a society that has failed to deliver a quarter of what their Western neighbours enjoy, made it clear that they sought union as quickly as possible. In the West the SPD changed sides, and found itself an ally in East Germany with the same name, and excellent prospects of winning the election there. The Greens, too, eventually bowed to the obvious sentiments of the East Germans.

In the past, the price demanded for German reunification by the Soviet Union was neutrality, the abandonment of Adenauer's adherence to the Atlantic Alliance. This price has been firmly rejected by successive West German governments, and today the Soviet Union is in no position to demand it. Its policy is to allow all its former satellites in the East self-determination. Western spokesmen have therefore made it clear that they expect a united Germany to remain in Nato; its membership of the EC has never been in question from either side.

Three issues need to be settled before German unity can be accepted and acknowledged by the international community, although *de facto* reunification may easily come first. The first is the question of security; the second that of Germany's borders; and the third the pace at which the present East Germany can be integrated into the EC.

The shape of a future security structure is the most difficult of these. To overcome the fact that both halves of Germany are today the most densely armed parts of the continent requires rapid progress at the CFE talks aimed at reducing those forces. But if the talks are to succeed and the agreed reductions to be implemented, the two alliances will have to continue in being. To dissolve them too soon would mean creating a whole new framework which would only delay the process.

The most likely outcome, therefore, is that for the moment final decisions about security will be set on one side, and integration at a monetary, economic and political level will take place first. During the first stages, Soviet troops will continue to be based in the East, but ultimately they will withdraw. Following a suggestion made by West German Foreign Minister Hans-Dietrich Genscher, it is not expected that allied forces will advance into East Germany after unification is complete. This would leave a united Germany in Nato, but with a declining number of US and other Nato troops on its soil, and with what was once East Germany effectively out of bounds. It is not a particularly tidy solution, but it will satisfy the 'realists' in the West without ruling out in the longer term the European security regime that many German politicians hanker after. Following discussions at a meeting of Nato and Warsaw Pact foreign ministers in Ottawa, it was agreed that the issue will be discussed at a meeting attended by the four victorious powers in World War II – the US, the USSR, Britain, and France – and the two existing German states: the so-called 4 plus 2 formula. It is not yet clear how strongly the Soviet Union will argue for a neutralised Germany at those talks, but the West will be at pains to establish that real Soviet interests would be best served by locking a united Germany solidly into Nato.

What any new arrangement must do is to contain German strength without exploiting Soviet weakness. A Germany detached from alliances is a more disconcerting prospect than one that remains anchored in Nato and the EC. Even Soviet interests would be better served by such an outcome than by an inchoate security structure in which the continent's major economic power has no clear locus. To concede Soviet demands for German neutrality would be an error, above all, for the Soviet Union itself.

Yet at the same time, the temptation to rub the Soviet Union's face in its own failure should be resisted. The most dangerous actor on the European stage would be a Soviet Union suffering from a 'Versailles complex' – a sense of defeat and national humiliation which could inspire a return to expansionism. For the moment, the Soviet people rightly blame 70 years of central planning and one-party rule for their problems, and the West must give them no excuse to change their minds and begin blaming outsiders.

The revolutions in Eastern Europe have torn up the maps by which European statesmen have navigated for the past 40 years. Few will regret their passing, for it was an era when peace was sustained through fear. But if we are to replace a stable system with one that is equally stable – yet does not depend on nuclear deterrence or the mutual balance of huge forces glaring at each other across the Iron Curtain – great ingenuity as well as statesmanship will be needed. The curtain has been torn down, and we can see each other clearly at last. Can we learn to live together in this more testing environment? That is the challenge ahead.